2

10A

14
31

1

Cove

WARSHIPS AND SUBMARINES
OF WORLD WAR II

WARSHIPS AND
SUBMARINES
OF WORLD WAR II

General Editor: Peter Darman

Grange
BOOKS

This edition published in 2004 by Grange Books
Grange Books plc
The Grange
1–6 Kingsnorth Estate
Hoo
Near Rochester
Kent ME3 9ND
www.grangebooks.co.uk

ISBN 1-84013-676-6

Printed in China

Editorial and design:
The Brown Reference Group plc
8 Chapel Place
Rivington Street
London
EC2A 3DQ
UK
www.brownreference.com

WARSHIPS
OF WORLD WAR II

CONTENTS

SUBMARINES
OF WORLD WAR II

CONTENTS

DUNKERQUE

SPECIFICATIONS

DUNKERQUE

Type: **Battleship**	Armour (deck): **139.7mm (5.5in)**
Length: **214.5m (703.75ft)**	Armour (turrets): **355.26mm (13.2in)**
Beam: **31.16m (102.25ft)**	Guns: **8x13in; 16x5.1in**
Draught: **8.68m (28.5ft)**	AA guns: **8x37mm; 32x13.2mm**
Displacement (normal): **26,924tnes (26,500t)**	Aircraft: **Two**
Displacement (full load): **36,068tnes (35,500t)**	Crew: **1431**
Machinery: **Steam Turbines**	Launched: **October 1935**
Armour (belt): **241.3mm (9.5in)**	Speed: **30 knots**

Launched on 2 October 1935 and completed in April 1937, *Dunkerque* was one of two new fast battleships on the French Navy's inventory in 1939, the other being the *Strasbourg*. At the outbreak of World War II in September 1939, these two vessels were the spearhead of a fast raiding force based at Brest, the battleships being supported by seven heavy cruisers, three light cruisers and some 50 destroyers.

This raiding force could achieve a speed of 30 knots, which at that time was not matched by any other naval force in the world. Dunkerque and her sister were modelled on the British "Nelson Class" and were fitted with a main armament of eight 330mm (13in) guns in two quadruple turrets.

On 3 July 1940, *Dunkerque* was moored in the Roads of Mers-el-Kebir and had begun to disarm, in accordance with the terms of the Armistice agreed between the Germans and the government of France, when she was attacked and severely damaged by British warships lying offshore. Three days later, she was further damaged during an attack by Royal Navy torpedo aircraft and partially sunk. After being refloated, she sailed for Toulon on 20 February 1942, and was scuttled there on 27 November that year when German forces occupied the port.

JEANNE D'ARC

The light cruiser *Jeanne D'Arc* was launched in February 1930 and completed in September 1931. The Armistice of June 1940 between the victorious Germans and the government of France found her in Martinique, where she was immobilized and disarmed on 1 May 1942 under the terms of an agreement signed between Admiral Robert, Governor of the island, and the US Government. The aircraft carrier *Bearn* and the light cruiser *Emile Bertin* were also decommissioned at this time. On 3 June 1943, Admiral Robert, who had remained loyal to the Vichy Government, turned Martinique over to the Free French Government in Algeria and made all three vessels available for war operations on the side of the Allies, providing much-needed firepower.

After refitting, during which her torpedo tubes were removed and her light armament modernised, *Jeanne D'Arc* took part in operations off Corsica and later formed part of the naval task force which shelled enemy positions along the Italian Riviera. She also carried out many transport operations, ferrying French troops and equipment from North Africa to the French Riviera after the Allied landings there in August 1944. *Jeanne D'Arc* served as a training ship postwar and remained on the French Navy's inventory until 1964.

SPECIFICATIONS

JEANNE D'ARC

Type: **Light Cruiser**	*Armour (deck):* **76mm (3in)**
Length: **170m (557.6ft)**	*Armour (turrets):* **95mm (3.75in)**
Beam: **17.5m (57.4ft)**	*Guns:* **8x155mm; 4x75mm**
Draught: **6.3m (20.6ft)**	*AA guns:* **4x37mm; 12x13.2mm**
Displacement (normal): **6600tnes (6496t)**	*Aircraft:* **One**
Displacement (full load): **9094tnes (8950t)**	*Crew:* **505**
Machinery: **Geared Turbines**	*Launched:* **February 1930**
Armour (belt): **120mm (4.75in)**	*Speed:* **25 knots**

MONTCALM

SPECIFICATIONS

MONTCALM

Type: **Light Cruiser**	*Armour (deck):* **50.8mm (2in)**
Length: **179m (587ft)**	*Armour (turrets):* **130mm (5in)**
Beam: **17.48m (57.3ft)**	*Guns:* **9x152mm**
Draught: **5.28m (17.3ft)**	*AA guns:* **8x90mm; 8x13.2mm**
Displacement (normal): **8342tnes (8214t)**	*Aircraft:* **Two**
Displacement (full load): **9266tnes (9120t)**	*Crew:* **540**
Machinery: **Boilers & Turbines**	*Launched:* **October 1935**
Armour (belt): **120mm (4.7in)**	*Speed:* **31 knots**

Launched in October 1935 and completed in December 1937, *Montcalm* was one of six light cruisers of the "La Galissonniere" class. The ships were very well designed and mounted an excellent main armament of nine 152mm (6in) guns. They were among the best in the French Navy, which was a world leader in military ships, at the outbreak of World War II in September 1939.

On 9 September 1940, *Montcalm,* accompanied by her sister ships *Marseillaise* and *Georges Leygues,* sailed from Toulon and reached Dakar, where they played their part in repulsing an unsuccessful attempt by British and Free French forces to take over the port on 23–25 September. In February 1943, after the French Command at Dakar joined the Allies, the three cruisers went to Philadelphia for a major refit, during which radar was installed and anti-aircraft armament increased.

On 6 June 1944, *Montcalm* and *Georges Leygues* formed part of the naval support force bombarding German shore positions at Omaha Beach during the invasion of Normandy, and in August they provided support for the Allied forces landing on the French Riviera. *Montcalm* and her sister vessels *Gloire* and *Georges Leygues* had active careers in the postwar French Navy; *Montcalm* herself was stricken in 1961.

RICHELIEU

The fast, modern battleship *Richelieu* was the leader of a class of three vessels, the others being the *Jean Bart* and *Clemenceau*. Launched in January 1939, the *Richelieu* escaped to Dakar in June 1940, and, on 8 July, she was damaged in a torpedo attack by British Fairey Swordfish carrier aircraft, her captain having refused demands to surrender or immobilize his ship. Despite being stranded in port, she used her 380mm (15in) guns to good advantage in beating off an attempt to capture Dakar by a combined Anglo/Free French force in September.

In January 1943, the French at Dakar having gone over to the Allies, she sailed for the United States to be repaired and refitted. In November 1943, she served briefly with the British Home Fleet before sailing for eastern waters in March 1944. On 25 July 1944, now serving with the British Eastern Fleet, she joined British warships in bombarding Sabang. From October 1944 to February 1945, she refitted at Casablanca, and in April 1945 she sailed for a second campaign with the Eastern Fleet.

After World War II she continued to serve the French Navy, and supported the French re-occupation of Indo-China in 1945-46. Placed in reserve in 1956, she was discarded in 1960 and broken up at the Italian port of La Spezia in 1968.

SPECIFICATIONS

RICHELIEU

Type: **Battleship**	Armour (deck): **170.18mm (6.7in)**
Length: **247.87 m (813.25ft)**	Armour (turrets): **429.26mm (16.9in)**
Beam: **33.14m (108.75ft)**	Guns: **8x15in; 9x6in; 12x3.9in**
Draught: **9.67m (31.75ft)**	AA guns: **16x37mm; 8x13.2mm**
Displacement (normal): **39,116tnes (38,500t)**	Aircraft: **Three**
Displacement (full load): **48,260tnes (47,500t)**	Crew: **1670**
Machinery: **Steam Turbines**	Launched: **January 1940**
Armour (belt): **345.44m (13.6in)**	Speed: **32 knots**

BISMARCK

SPECIFICATIONS

BISMARCK

Type: **Battleship**	Armour (deck): **80mm (3.15in)**
Length: **251m (823.5ft)**	Armour (turrets): **360mm (14.2in)**
Beam: **35.96m (118ft)**	Guns: **8x15in; 12x5.9in**
Draught: **9.54m (31.3ft)**	AA guns: **14x4.1in; 16x37mm**
Displacement (normal): **46,923tnes (45,200t)**	Aircraft: **Six**
Displacement (full load): **51,763tnes (50,950t)**	Crew: **2100**
Machinery: **Steam Turbines**	Launched: **February 1939**
Armour (belt): **68mm (12.6in)**	Speed: **30 knots**

Together with her sister ship, *Tirpitz*, the *Bismarck* was the pride of Hitler's navy, and was viewed with alarm by the Royal Navy. Launched in February 1939 and completed in August 1940, she underwent sea trials in the Baltic and in May 1941 she sailed in company with the heavy cruiser *Prinz Eugen* to attack Allied commerce in the Atlantic.

Detected by British aircraft, the German warships were intercepted by units of the British Home Fleet in the Denmark Strait, between Greenland and Iceland, and a running battle developed during which the *Bismarck* sank the battlecruiser HMS *Hood* and damaged the battleship *Prince of Wales*. Hits on the *Bismarck* reduced her speed, though, and produced an oil slick in her wake.

On 26 May she was attacked by Swordfish aircraft from the carrier *Ark Royal*; a torpedo hit destroyed her steering gear and rendered her unmanoeuvrable. On 27 May she was shelled to pieces by the battleships *King George V* and *Rodney*, her crew resisting until the last. Finished off by torpedoes and gunfire, she sank some 480km (300 miles) northwest of Brest with the loss of 1977 officers and men – a grievous loss to the German Navy. Half a century later, her wreck was photographed by a miniature submarine.

BLÜCHER

Launched in June 1937, the heavy cruiser *Blücher* was one of five vessels in her class, the others being the *Lützow, Seydlitz, Prinz Eugen* and *Admiral Hipper*. On 9 April 1940, flying the flag of Admiral Oskar Kummetz, she took part in the German invasion of Norway, leading a group of warships carrying 2000 troops and bound for the Norwegian capital, Oslo.

This spearhead force was to be followed by 15 transport vessels, carrying a further 3761 troops. Although the invasion – the first major amphibious operation of World War II – was meticulously well planned, Admiral Kummetz ordered his force to proceed through the Drobak Narrows, leading to Oslofjord, at only 12 knots. This would prove a costly decision for the German Navy. The waterway was only 457m (500yd) wide and was heavily defended by forts. Holding their fire until the Blücher was at point-blank range, the Norwegian gunners opened fire and quickly set her ablaze. Their torpedoes then reduced her to a helpless hulk, and at 06:30 hours she capsized and sank with the loss of over 1000 officers and men.

In the 1990s, fuel oil leaking from her corroded tanks began to pose a serious pollution threat, requiring a major underwater engineering effort in order to avert a large-scale environmental disaster.

SPECIFICATIONS

BLÜCHER

Type: **Heavy Cruiser**	*Armour (deck):* **50.8mm (2in)**
Length: **205.83m (675.3ft)**	*Armour (turrets):* **101.6mm (4in)**
Beam: **21.25m (69.75ft)**	*Guns:* **8x8in; 12x4.1in**
Draught: **5.79m (19ft)**	*AA guns:* **12x40mm; 8x37mm**
Displacement (normal): **14,474tnes (14,247t)**	*Aircraft:* **Three**
Displacement (full load): **18,499tnes (18,208t)**	*Crew:* **1600**
Machinery: **Boilers & Steam Turbines**	*Launched:* **June 1937**
Armour (belt): **76.2mm (3in)**	*Speed:* **32.5 knots**

EMDEN

SPECIFICATIONS

EMDEN

Type: **Light Cruiser**	Armour (deck): **38.1mm (1.5in)**
Length: **155m (508.75ft)**	Armour (conning tower): **101.6mm (4in)**
Beam: **14.32m (47ft)**	Guns: **8x5.9in; 3x3.5in**
Draught: **5.15m (16.9ft)**	AA guns: **2x40mm; 20x20mm**
Displacement (normal): **5780tnes (5689t)**	Aircraft: **None**
Displacement (full load): **7215tnes (7102t)**	Crew: **630**
Machinery: **Boilers & Steam Turbines**	Launched: **January 1925**
Armour (belt): **50.8mm (2in)**	Speed: **29 knots**

Completed in January 1925, the light cruiser *Emden* was the first medium-sized German warship built after World War I. Originally a coal-burning vessel, she was intended primarily for overseas service and consequently had a large bunker capacity; particular attention was paid to accommodation space and crew comfort, something of a novelty at that time. Her first mission in World War II was to lay mines in the North Sea, and, in April 1940, she was one of the warships that accompanied the *Blücher* during the invasion of Norway. Though this operation was a costly affair in terms of shipping, she survived and was later transferred to the Baltic and saw considerable operational service there, initially operating as part of a powerful task force that included the new battleship *Tirpitz* and later operating as a mine warfare training vessel.

In late 1944 and early 1945 she was involved in evacuating troops and civilians from East Prussia in the face of the Russian advance; one of her more unusual tasks, in January 1945, was to evacuate the coffin containing the body of Field Marshal von Hindenburg, which had been interred at the Tannenberg Memorial, from *Königsberg*. In April 1945 Emden was damaged in a bombing attack on Kiel. She was scuttled and broken up in 1949.

GNEISENAU

The battlecruiser *Gneisenau* was launched in December 1936 and completed in May 1938. She was upgraded in the following year and made her first Atlantic sortie, with her sister ship, *Scharnhorst*, in November 1939, sinking the British auxiliary cruiser *Rawalpindi*. She was damaged by gunfire from the British battlecruiser *Renown* off Norway on 9 April 1940, but on 8 June she and *Scharnhorst* sank the British aircraft carrier *Glorious* and her escorting destroyers *Ardent* and *Acasta*. On 20 June 1940 she was torpedoed by the Royal Navy submarine HMS *Clyde* off Trondheim. In January 1941, again with the *Scharnhorst*, she made another sortie into the Atlantic, the two sinking 22 merchant ships – a moderately successful action.

On 6 April 1941 she was torpedoed by a British aircraft at Brest, and further damaged by aircraft bombs four days later. In February 1942, with the *Scharnhorst* and the heavy cruiser *Prinz Eugen*, she made the famous dash through the English Channel from Brest to Germany, being damaged by a mine en route. On 27 February 1942 she was damaged by bombs at Kiel, after which her guns were removed and she was decommissioned. She was towed to Gdynia and sunk as a blockship there in March 1945. Her hulk was broken up in 1947–51.

SPECIFICATIONS

GNEISENAU

Type: **Battlecruiser**	Armour (deck): **50.8mm (2in)**
Length: **229.74m (753.75ft)**	Armour (turrets): **360.68mm (14.2in)**
Beam: **30m (98.3ft)**	Guns: **9x11in; 12x5.9in; 14x4in**
Draught: **8.68m (28.5ft)**	AA guns: **16x37mm; 8x20mm**
Displacement (normal): **35,407tnes (34,850t)**	Aircraft: **Three**
Displacement (full load): **39522tnes (38,900t)**	Crew: **1670**
Machinery: **Steam Turbines**	Launched: **December 1936**
Armour (belt): **350.5mm (13.8in)**	Speed: **31.5 knots**

GRAF SPEE

SPECIFICATIONS

GRAF SPEE

Type: **Pocket Battleship**	Armour (deck): **40.64mm (1.6in)**
Length: **187.9m (616.5ft)**	Armour (turrets): **139.7mm (5.5in)**
Beam: **21.64m (71ft)**	Guns: **6x11in; 8x5.9in; 6x3.5in**
Draught: **7.31m (24ft)**	AA guns: **None**
Displacement (normal): **13,818tnes (13,600t)**	Aircraft: **Two**
Displacement (full load): **16,279tnes (16,023t)**	Crew: **1150**
Machinery: **Diesel**	Launched: **June 1934**
Armour (belt): **58.42mm (2.3in)**	Speed: **26 knots**

Officially classed as a Panzerschiff (Armoured Ship), but more popularly known as a "pocket battleship", the *Admiral Graf Spee* and her two sisters, the *Admiral Scheer* and *Deutschland*, were designed as commerce raiders with a large radius of action and complied with the restrictions imposed on Germany by the terms of the Treaty of Versailles (which was detested by the Nazi Party). The "pocket battleship" nickname derived from the fact that, although they were too small to be classed as battleships, they were more powerful and faster than most other warships then afloat. Their hulls were electrically welded, and armour protection was sacrificed to produce a higher speed.

The *Graf Spee* was launched in June 1934 and completed in January 1936. In 1936–37, during the Spanish Civil War, she was engaged in blockading Republican ports. Between September and November 1939, during a sortie into the South Atlantic, she sank or captured nine British merchant vessels before being brought to battle by a British naval force comprising the cruisers *Exeter*, *Ajax* and *Achilles* off the estuary of the River Plate. Forced to seek refuge in the neutral port of Montevideo, on 17 December she was scuttled; her captain, Hans Langsdorff, committed suicide rather than be taken prisoner.

KÖLN

Completed in May 1928, *Köln* was one of a class of three light cruisers in the German Navy, the others being the *Königsberg* and *Karlsruhe*. *Köln* was in action from the very first day of World War II, taking part in minelaying operations in the North Sea with Admiral Densch's Reconnaissance Force.

During the invasion of Norway in April 1940, she and the *Königsberg* formed part of the naval force covering the German landing at Bergen. *Köln* remained in northern waters until 1943, when she was transferred to the Baltic Fleet. She subsequently took part in many operations in support of German forces, and from late 1944, while serving with the Fleet Training Squadron, she was heavily involved in evacuating civilian and military personnel from East Prussia, a mission of some risk though one she performed very well.

On 30 March 1945, only a few weeks away from the end of the war, while undergoing a refit, she was badly damaged in a heavy attack on Wilhelmshaven Naval Dockyard by B-24 bombers of the United States Army Air Force (USAAF), settling on the bottom with only her superstructure above the surface. She was decommissioned on 6 April 1945, although her guns were still intact and she was used for local defence until the German surrender. She was scrapped in 1946.

SPECIFICATIONS

KÖLN

Type: **Light Cruiser**	*Armour (deck):* **38.1mm (1.5in)**
Length: **173.95m (570.75ft)**	*Armour (turrets):* **25.4mm (1in)**
Beam: **15.24m (50ft)**	*Guns:* **9x5.9in; 6x3.46in**
Draught: **5.58m (18.3ft)**	*AA guns:* **8x37mm**
Displacement (normal): **6864tnes (6756t)**	*Aircraft:* **Two**
Displacement (full load): **8392tnes (8260t)**	*Crew:* **820**
Machinery: **Boilers & Steam Turbines**	*Launched:* **May 1928**
Armour (belt): **68.58mm (2.7in)**	*Speed:* **32 knots**

LÜTZOW

SPECIFICATIONS

LÜTZOW

Type: **Pocket Battleship**	*Armour (deck):* **40.64mm (1.6in)**
Length: **187.9m (616.5ft)**	*Armour (turrets):* **139.7mm (5.5in)**
Beam: **21.33m (70ft)**	*Guns:* **6x11in; 8x5.9in**
Draught: **7.23m (23.75ft)**	*AA guns:* **6x3.46in**
Displacement (normal): **13,817tnes (13,600t)**	*Aircraft:* **Two**
Displacement (full load): **15,670tnes (15,423t)**	*Crew:* **1150**
Machinery: **Diesels**	*Launched:* **May 1931**
Armour (belt): **58.42mm (2.3in)**	*Speed:* **26 knots**

Originally named *Deutschland*, the *Lützow* was one of three armoured ships – the so-called "pocket battleships" – laid down between 1928 and 1931. *Deutschland* was the first of the class, being launched in May 1931 and completed in April 1933. She was originally used as a seagoing training ship, to familiarize crews with her new technology.

On 22 May 1937 she was damaged by bombs dropped by a Spanish Republican aircraft off Ibiza, 22 of her crew being killed. In October 1939, after the outbreak of World War II, she made a sortie into the Atlantic, sinking two merchant ships and capturing a third. On 15 November 1939 she was renamed Lützow, and in February 1940 she was reclassified as a heavy cruiser. During the invasion of Norway in April 1940 she was damaged by shore batteries and by a torpedo from the British submarine Spearfish.

On 13 June 1941 she was again badly damaged by a torpedo from a British aircraft off Norway. After repair, she remained in Norwegian waters in 1942–43 and then went to Gdynia for a refit, subsequently providing fire support for German forces in the Baltic area. On 16 April 1945 she was bombed and sunk by British aircraft, who were roaming the skies of Germany at will, in shallow water at Swinemunde.

PRINZ EUGEN

The *Prinz Eugen*, launched in August 1938, was the third of five heavy cruisers laid down for the Kriegsmarine in the 1930s. On 23 April 1941 she was damaged by a magnetic mine, but was repaired in time to sail for the Atlantic with the battleship *Bismarck* in May. *Prinz Eugen* managed to elude the British warships hunting the *Bismarck,* having been detached to make her own way to the French Atlantic ports, and so escaped *Bismarck*'s fate, arriving at Brest on 1 June 1941 undamaged. On 12 February 1942 she took part in the famous "Channel Dash" with the battlecruisers *Scharnhorst* and *Gneisenau,* which totally humiliated the Royal Navy.

She subsequently saw service in the Baltic with the Fleet Training Squadron, and in 1944 provided fire support to German forces resisting the Soviet advance. On 15 October 1944 she was badly damaged in collision with the light cruiser *Leipzig.*

The end of World War II found her at Copenhagen, where she surrendered to the Allies. She was allocated to the United States and was used as a target vessel in the atomic bomb tests at Bikini Atoll in 1946, which she survived in a badly damaged condition. Her hulk was finally sunk by American warships at Kwajalein on 15 November 1947.

SPECIFICATIONS

PRINZ EUGEN

Type: **Heavy Cruiser**	*Armour (deck):* **50.8mm (2in)**
Length: **212.44m (697ft)**	*Armour (turrets):* **101.6mm (4in)**
Beam: **21.8m (71.5ft)**	*Guns:* **8x8in; 12x4.1in**
Draught: **7.16m (23.5ft)**	*AA guns:* **12x40mm; 8x37mm**
Displacement (normal): **14,500tnes (14,271t)**	*Aircraft:* **Three**
Displacement (full load): **19,000tnes (18,700t)**	*Crew:* **1600**
Machinery: **Boilers & Steam Turbines**	*Launched:* **August 1938**
Armour (belt): **76.2mm (3in)**	*Speed:* **33 knots**

SCHARNHORST

SPECIFICATIONS

SCHARNHORST

Type: **Battlecruiser**	Armour (deck): **50.8mm (2in)**
Length: **230.96m (757.75ft)**	Armour (turrets): **360.68mm (14.2in)**
Beam: **30m (898.4ft)**	Guns: **9x11in; 12x5.9in; 14x4in**
Draught: **8.68m (28.5ft)**	AA guns: **16x37mm**
Displacement (normal): **35,408tnes (34,850t)**	Aircraft: **Three**
Displacement (full load): **39,522tnes (38,900t)**	Crew: **1670**
Machinery: **Steam Turbines**	Launched: **October 1936**
Armour (belt): **350.5mm (13.8in)**	Speed: **31.5 knots**

Laid down at Wilhelmshaven in April 1934 and launched in October 1936, the *Scharnhorst* and her sister ship *Gneisenau* were modelled on the uncompleted "Mackensen" class battlecruisers of World War I. Up until 1942 the pair operated as a single battle group, but after the "Channel Dash" of February that year – in which *Scharnhorst* was mined twice while en route from Brest to Kiel – she operated alone.

In January 1943, after repair, *Scharnhorst* was sent to Norway with the heavy cruiser *Prinz Eugen*, the two ships operating from Altenfjord together with the battleship *Tirpitz* and the heavy cruiser *Lützow*. In September 1943 *Scharnhorst* and *Tirpitz* bombarded shore installations on Spitzbergen, and on 25 December *Scharnhorst* sailed to intercept an Allied convoy (JW55B) heading from Scotland to Kola, in north Russia. However, the result was that she herself became the prey, for on the following day the German battlecruiser was intercepted off Norway's North Cape by a force of British cruisers and destroyers, which inflicted some damage on her after a brief action. Gunfire from the battleship *Duke of York* and torpedoes from the destroyers then reduced her to a blazing wreck. Even so, she fought on with her surviving armament until she finally blew up and sank that evening.

SCHLESWIG-HOLSTEIN

The *Schleswig-Holstein* was one of a class of five pre-dreadnought battleships, laid down in 1902–04. She was launched in December 1906, completed in July 1908 and subsequently served with the German High Seas Fleet, seeing action in the Battle of Jutland. In the last two years of the war she served in turn as a depot ship at Bremerhaven and an accommodation ship at Kiel, and was one of the small force of warships that Germany was permitted to retain by the Versailles Treaty for coastal defence in the post-war years.

After substantial reconstruction, she was used as a cadet training ship. In August 1939 she was brought back into firstline service to provide fire support for German forces invading Poland, and on 1 September her four 280mm (11in) guns fired the opening shots of World War II when she shelled the Polish fortress of Westerplatte (she was in the area on a goodwill visit. She continued the bombardment for a week, until the Polish garrison surrendered on 7 September.

She later led a battle group covering troop transports in the invasion of Norway in 1940, before returning to the Baltic to reassume her role as a training vessel. On 18 December 1944 she was severely damaged in an RAF bombing raid on Gdynia, and was finally scuttled on 21 March 1945.

SPECIFICATIONS

SCHLESWIG-HOLSTEIN

Type: **Pre-Dreadnought**	Armour (deck): **38.1mm (1.5in)**
Length: **127.55m (418.5ft)**	Armour (turrets): **279.4mm (11in)**
Beam: **22.12m (72.6ft)**	Guns: **4x11in;14x6.7in;20x3.5in**
Draught: **8.22m (27ft)**	AA guns: **None**
Displacement (normal): **13,400tnes (13,190t)**	Aircraft: **None**
Displacement (full load): **14,441tnes (14,220t)**	Crew: **745**
Machinery: **Boilers**	Launched: **December 1906**
Armour (belt): **228.6mm (9in)**	Speed: **18 knots**

TIRPITZ

SPECIFICATIONS

TIRPITZ

Type: **Battleship**	Armour (deck): **80mm (3.15in)**
Length: **251m (823.5ft)**	Armour (turrets): **360.68mm (14.2in)**
Beam: **36m (118ft)**	Guns: **8x15in; 12x5.9in; 16x4.1in**
Draught: **9.45m (31ft)**	AA guns: **16x37mm**
Displacement (normal): **45,923tnes (45,200t)**	Aircraft: **Six**
Displacement (full load): **51,765tnes (50,950t)**	Crew: **2100**
Machinery: **Steam Turbines**	Launched: **April 1939**
Armour (belt): **320mm (12.6in)**	Speed: **30 knots**

The mighty battleship *Tirpitz* was laid down in October 1936 and was originally known as *Schlachtschiff G* or *Ersatz Schleswig-Holstein* (Replacement Schleswig-Holstein). She was launched on 1 April 1939 and completed in February 1941.

From early 1942 she was based at various locations in Norway, and on 8 September 1943 she sailed from Altenfjord to bombard shore installations on Spitzbergen – the only time she fired her guns in anger against a surface target. On 22 September she was damaged in an attack by British midget submarines, and on 3 April 1944 she was further damaged in an attack by carrier aircraft of the British Fleet Air Arm, sustaining 14 bomb hits and suffering 122 dead. She was subjected to further attacks by the Fleet Air Arm in August 1944, but sustained only minor bomb hits.

On 15 September 1944, however, she was attacked by RAF Lancasters while at anchor in Tromsö and was damaged by one of the RAF's new 5443kg (12,000lb) "Tallboy" deep penetration bombs. She was now no longer seaworthy, but on 12 November 1944 she was again attacked by Lancasters carrying 'Tallboy" bombs and received two direct hits, capsizing with the loss of 902 officers and men. Her hulk was gradually cut up over the next 12 years.

ARGONAUT

Built by Cammell Laird and launched in September 1941, HMS *Argonaut* was one of 16 "Dido"-class light cruisers completed for the British Royal Navy between 1939 and 1942.

After service with the Home Fleet, she was transferred to Gibraltar for service with Force H and took part in Operation Torch, the Allied landings in North Africa in November 1942. After refitting in the United States in 1943, she returned to the Home Fleet in time to participate in the Normandy landings on 6 June 1944, forming part of the maritime support force for the landing on "Gold" Beach, and in August she lent fire support during the Allied landings on the French Riviera. In September-October 1944 she formed part of the naval force covering Allied landings in Greece and the Aegean Islands, after which she sailed to join the Eastern Fleet in Ceylon.

In December 1944 and January 1945 she covered British carrier task forces attacking targets in Sumatra, after which she deployed to the Pacific as part of the British Pacific Fleet. She remained operational in the Pacific for the rest of the war, covering the British Task Force 37 operating off Okinawa and the Japanese Home Islands. *Argonaut* was finally scrapped at Newport in November 1955.

SPECIFICATIONS

ARGONAUT

Type: **Light Cruiser**	*Armour (deck):* **50.8mm (2in)**
Length: **156m (512ft)**	*Armour (turrets):* **38.1mm (1.5in)**
Beam: **15.24m (50ft)**	*Guns:* **10x5.25in**
Draught: **5.18m (17ft)**	*AA guns:* **8x2pdr; 8x.5in**
Displacement (normal): **5933tnes (5840t)**	*Aircraft:* **None**
Displacement (full load): **7193tnes (7080t)**	*Crew:* **487**
Machinery: **Steam Turbines**	*Launched:* **September 1941**
Armour (belt): **38.1mm (1.5in)**	*Speed:* **31.75 knots**

AJAX

SPECIFICATIONS

AJAX

Type: **Light Cruiser**	Armour (deck): **50.8mm (2in)**
Length: **168.85m (554ft)**	Armour (turrets): **25.4mm (1in)**
Beam: **16.76m (55ft)**	Guns: **8x6in; 4x4in**
Draught: **6.03m (19.8ft)**	AA guns: **12x.5in**
Displacement (normal): **7549tnes (7430t)**	Aircraft: **One**
Displacement (full load): **9500tnes (9350t)**	Crew: **570**
Machinery: **Steam Turbines**	Launched: **September 1932**
Armour (belt): **88.9mm (3.5in)**	Speed: **32.5 knots**

A "Leander"-class light cruiser, built by Vickers-Armstrong and launched in March 1934, HMS *Ajax* was in the South Atlantic on anti-commerce raider duty in the weeks following the outbreak of World War II in September 1939. In December 1939, together with the cruisers *Exeter* and *Achilles,* she intercepted and engaged the German pocket battleship *Admiral Graf Spee* off the estuary of the River Plate, being severely damaged in the action (the action was made famous in the film *The Battle of the River Plate*). After substantial repairs, she deployed to the Mediterranean, where she took part in convoy escort duty.

On 28 May 1941 she was damaged by German dive-bombers while en route to take part in the evacuation of British and Greek forces from the island of Crete, and was again damaged by air attack off the Algerian coast in January 1943. At the D-Day landings, the invasion of Normandy, in June 1944, she joined the cruisers *Argonaut, Orion* and *Emerald* in providing fire support for the assault on "Gold" Beach; she also covered the Allied landings in southern France in August.

In September-October 1944 she operated in the Aegean. She remained with the Mediterranean Fleet for the remainder of the war and was scrapped in November 1949.

ARK ROYAL

L aid down at the Cammell Laird Shipyard in September 1934, the aircraft carrier *Ark Royal* combined the best features of previous designs, incorporating a full-length flight deck overhanging the stern. Launched on 13 April 1937 and completed in November 1938, she was employed in the search for German vessels attempting to reach their home ports at the outbreak of World War II, during which operations she narrowly escaped being torpedoed by a U-boat.

In April 1940 her aircraft provided cover for Allied forces during the evacuation of Norway. In July 1940 her aircraft carried out attacks on French warships at Mers-el-Kebir, and later in the year she carried out convoy protection duty in the Mediterranean. In May 1941 she took part in the hunt for the *Bismarck*, her Swordfish aircraft achieving torpedo hits that sent the warship out of control and directly led to her destruction.

In the following months, on several occasions, she flew off reinforcement aircraft for the besieged island of Malta. These were dangerous missions, as Axis aircraft and submarines were very active at this time. It was after one such operation, as she was heading back to Gibraltar on 13 November 1941, that she was hit by the submarine *U81*. She sank under tow the next day, for the loss of only one life.

SPECIFICATIONS

ARK ROYAL

Type: **Aircraft Carrier**	*Armour (deck):* **88.9mm (3.5in)**
Length: **243.84m (800ft)**	*Armour (turrets):* **N/A**
Beam: **28.65m (94ft)**	*Guns:* **16x4.5in**
Draught: **8.53m (28ft)**	*AA guns:* **32x2pdr; 32x.5in**
Displacement (normal): **23,978tnes (23,600t)**	*Aircraft:* **60**
Displacement (full load): **28,936tnes (28,480t)**	*Crew:* **1600**
Machinery: **Steam Turbines**	*Launched:* **April 1937**
Armour (belt): **24.3mm (4.5in)**	*Speed:* **32 knots**

AUDACITY

SPECIFICATIONS

AUDACITY

Type: **Escort Carrier**	Armour (deck): **None**
Length: **142.3m (467ft)**	Armour (turrets): **N/A**
Beam: **17.06m (56ft)**	Guns: **1x4in**
Draught: **8.38m (27.5ft)**	AA guns: **6x20mm**
Displacement (normal): **Unknown**	Aircraft: **Eight**
Displacement (full load): **11,172tnes (11,000t)**	Crew: **650**
Machinery: **Diesel Turbines**	Launched: **March 1939**
Armour (belt): **None**	Speed: **16 knots**

HMS *Audacity*, the Royal Navy's first escort carrier, was a conversion of the German merchant vessel *Hannover*, captured in the West Indies in February 1940. Conversion was completed in June 1941, and from September she was used on the UK-Gibraltar route, her American-built Grumman Martlet fighters proving of great value in scouting for enemy submarines and fighting off the Focke-Wulf Condor maritime reconnaissance aircraft which, in the first half of 1941, had sunk a greater tonnage of Allied shipping than any other Axis aircraft or vessel, including the deadly U-boats. One of *Audacity*'s Martlets actually shot down a Condor on 21 September, during the carrier's first operational voyage.

During her final voyage, which began on 14 December 1941, no fewer than four Condors were destroyed by the carrier's Martlets, and her Swordfish made attacks on enemy U-boats, one of which, the *U131*, was unable to submerge as a result and had to be scuttled when British warships approached. However, on the night of 22–23 December *Audacity* was torpedoed and sunk by the *U751*. She was the forerunner of many escort carriers, which were to contribute greatly to the defeat of the U-boats during the strategically vital Battle of the Atlantic.

BARHAM

HMS *Barham* was one of five fast battleships of the "Queen Elizabeth" class, laid down in 1912–13 to replace battlecruisers as the offensive element of the battle fleet.

Launched in December 1914 and completed in October 1915, *Barham* served with the Grand Fleet throughout World War I and saw action at Jutland, where she received six hits. Reconstructed in 1927–28, she served in the Mediterranean until 1939, when she was assigned to the Home Fleet. On 12 December 1939 she sank the destroyer *Duchess* in a collision off the west coast of Scotland. Her bad luck continued to dog her, as a fortnight later she was damaged by a torpedo from the *U30* off the Clyde estuary.

Reassigned to the Mediterranean Fleet after repair, she was damaged by gunfire from the French battleship *Richelieu* during the Anglo-French attack on Dakar, and was again damaged by air attack off Crete on 27 May 1941, during the German airborne invasion of the island. She took part in several shore bombardment operations, her 381mm (15in) guns being used to good effect against enemy installations at Bardia, Libya. On 25 November 1941 she was torpedoed three times by the *U331*, capsized and blew up off Sollum, Egypt, with the loss of 862 lives.

SPECIFICATIONS

BARHAM

Type: **Battleship**	*Armour (deck):* **76.2mm (3in)**
Length: **196m (643ft)**	*Armour (turrets):* **330.2mm (13in)**
Beam: **31.7m (104ft)**	*Guns:* **8x15in; 4x6in**
Draught: **10.41m (34.1ft)**	*AA guns:* **2x4in**
Displacement (normal): **29,616tnes (29,150t)**	*Aircraft:* **2–3**
Displacement (full load): **33,528tnes (33,000t)**	*Crew:* **1297**
Machinery: **Steam Turbines**	*Launched:* **December 1914**
Armour (belt): **330.2mm (13in)**	*Speed:* **25 knots**

BELFAST

SPECIFICATIONS

BELFAST

Type: **Heavy Cruiser**	Armour (deck): **76.2mm (3in)**
Length: **186.8m (613ft)**	Armour (turrets): **101.6mm (4in)**
Beam: **19.2m (63ft)**	Guns: **12x6in; 12x4in**
Draught: **6m (20ft)**	AA guns: **16x2pdr; 8x.5in**
Displacement (normal): **10,805tnes (10,635t)**	Aircraft: **Three**
Displacement (full load): **13,386tnes (13,175t)**	Crew: **780**
Machinery: **Steam Turbines**	Launched: **March 1938**
Armour (belt): **123.9mm (4.88in)**	Speed: **33 knots**

The cruiser HMS *Belfast* and her sister ship, *Edinburgh*, were both laid down in December 1936 and launched in March 1938. *Belfast* was the larger of the two; in fact, she was the largest cruiser ever built for the Royal Navy.

Belfast suffered an early misfortune when, in November 1939, she was badly damaged by a magnetic mine, which exploded beneath the forward engine room, breaking her back and fracturing all the machinery mountings. She returned to service in October 1942, having undergone a number of modifications, and was assigned to Arctic convoy escort duty. In December 1943 she took part in the Battle of North Cape, which culminated in the destruction of the German Navy battlecruiser *Scharnhorst*.

On 6 June 1944 she formed part of the naval force assigned to support the Allied landing on "Juno" Beach in Normandy, and on the 26th she joined other warships in bombarding German positions in the Caen area. *Belfast* continued to serve for many years postwar; she was refitted in 1963 and placed in reserve, being designated a headquarters ship in 1966. In 1971 she was preserved as a permanent memorial, being moored at Simon's Wharf on the River Thames. She continues to be a popular tourist attraction.

CENTURION

HMS *Centurion* was a dreadnought of the 1910 "King George V" class. She was laid down at Devonport in January 1911 and launched in November of that year. On 9 December 1912 she sank the Italian steamer *Derna* in a collision while on her sea trials. Completed in May 1913, she served with the Grand Fleet for the duration of World War I and saw action at the indecisive Battle of Jutland in 1916.

From 1919 to 1924 she served in the Mediterranean and the Black Sea, after which she was converted as a remotely-controlled target ship.

In 1939–40 she underwent another conversion, being modified to resemble the battleship HMS *Anson*. She retained this role until 1942, being transferred to Alexandria, and in June 1942 she made an operational sortie as part of a force running supplies through to Alexandria to Malta (Operation Vigorous). By this stage of her career, though, she was rather obsolete and very vulnerable to air attack.

She subsequently served as a floating anti-aircraft battery, being anchored south of Suez. Reduced to Care and Maintenance status, she made her last voyage in June 1944, proceeding to the English Channel to be sunk off Normandy on 9 June to form a breakwater as part of an artificial harbour.

SPECIFICATIONS

CENTURION

Type: **Battleship**	Armour (deck): **102mm (4in)**
Length: **181.2m (597.6ft)**	Armour (turrets): **279mm (11in)**
Beam: **27.1m (89ft)**	Guns: **10x343mm**
Draught: **8.7m (28.75ft)**	AA guns: **4x102mm**
Displacement (normal): **23,369tnes (23,000t)**	Aircraft: **None**
Displacement (full load): **26,112tnes (25,700t)**	Crew: **782**
Machinery: **Four Turbines**	Launched: **November 1911**
Armour (belt): **305mm (12in)**	Speed: **21.75 knots**

DUKE OF YORK

SPECIFICATIONS

DUKE OF YORK

Type: **Battleship**	*Armour (deck):* **152.4mm (6in)**
Length: **227m (745ft)**	*Armour (turrets):* **330.2mm (13in)**
Beam: **31.39m (103ft)**	*Guns:* **10x14in; 15x5.25in**
Draught: **9.6m (31.5ft)**	*AA guns:* **64x2pdr**
Displacement (normal): **38,608tnes (38,000t)**	*Aircraft:* **Two**
Displacement (full load): **45,517tnes (44,800t)**	*Crew:* **1900**
Machinery: **Steam Turbines**	*Launched:* **February 1940**
Armour (belt): **381mm (15in)**	*Speed:* **29 knots**

One of five battleships that formed the 1936 "King George V" class, the *Duke of York* – originally laid down as the *Anson* and renamed in 1938 – was launched in February 1940 and completed in November 1941, a month before her sister ship, *Prince of Wales*, was sunk by Japanese air attack off Malaya.

One of the new battleship's first tasks was to carry the British Prime Minister, Winston Churchill, across the Atlantic for a meeting with US President Franklin D. Roosevelt in December 1941. From 1942 she was employed primarily on convoy protection duties in Atlantic and Arctic waters during the Battle of the Atlantic, but in November 1942 she joined the battleships *Nelson* and *Rodney* in providing fire support for the Allied landings in North Africa.

In December 1943 her gunfire was instrumental in the destruction of the German battlecruiser *Scharnhorst* off North Cape, the enemy warship being finished off by torpedo attacks. In 1945, after a refit, she sailed to join the British Pacific Fleet, arriving in August, too late to participate in the hostilities (where she would have provided support for the invasion of the Japanese home lands). In November 1951 the *Duke of York* was laid up in reserve, and in 1958 she was broken up at Faslane, Scotland.

DUNEDIN

Hms *Dunedin* was one of a class of eight light cruisers launched at the close of, or just after, World War I. Most served in the Far East, the South Atlantic or the Mediterranean. *Dunedin* herself was launched on 19 November 1918 and was loaned to the Royal New Zealand Navy between 1924 and 1937, along with a sister ship, *Diomede*.

Reassigned to the Royal Navy before the outbreak of World War II, she formed part of the Northern Patrol from 6 September 1939, searching for enemy vessels attempting to reach Germany. In 1940 she was assigned to convoy escort duty, and in June 1941 she captured the German supply ship *Lothringen*, stationed in the Atlantic to replenish U-boats operating off Freetown, Sierra Leone. In the weeks that followed she captured two Vichy French steamers.

On 24 November, 1941, she was searching for U-boats sent to assist the German commerce raider *Atlantis* when she was sighted by the German submarine *U124* (commanded by)Lt Cdr Mohr) which torpedoed and sank her. She was the only one of her class to be lost through enemy action in World War II; the others were scrapped after the war with the exception of HMS *Dragon*, sunk as a breakwater off Normandy to form part of an artificial harbour.

SPECIFICATIONS

DUNEDIN

Type: **Light Cruiser**	Armour (deck): **25.4mm (1in)**
Length: **143.86m (472ft)**	Armour (turrets): **25.4mm (1in)**
Beam: **14m (46ft)**	Guns: **6x6in; 2x3in**
Draught: **4.87m (16ft)**	AA guns: **2x2pdr**
Displacement (normal): **4663tnes (4590t)**	Aircraft: **None**
Displacement (full load): **5811tnes (5720t)**	Crew: **450**
Machinery: **Steam Turbines**	Launched: **November 1918**
Armour (belt): **76.2mm (3in)**	Speed: **30 knots**

EDINBURGH

SPECIFICATIONS

EDINBURGH

Type:	Armour (deck):
Cruiser	**76.2mm (3in)**

Length:	Armour (turrets):
18.7m (613ft)	**101.6mm (4in)**

Beam:	Guns:
19.2m (63ft)	**12x6in; 12x4in**

Draught:	AA guns:
8.83m (29ft)	**16x2pdr; 8x.5in**

Displacement (normal):	Aircraft:
10,805tnes (10,635t)	**Three**

Displacement (full load):	Crew:
13,386tnes (13,175t)	**780**

Machinery:	Launched:
Steam Turbines	**March 1938**

Armour (belt):	Speed:
124mm (4.88in)	**33 knots**

The cruiser HMS *Edinburgh* was launched on 31 March 1938, a fortnight after her sister ship, HMS *Belfast*. Both vessels spent the early weeks of World War II searching for German blockade runners, heading homewards via the Norwegian Sea.

In 1940 her main role was convoy protection, but in 1941 she made an occasional foray into the Arctic to hunt down German weather observation ships. In May 1941 she took part in the hunt for the German battleship *Bismarck*, and in July she was deployed to the Mediterranean for convoy escort duty, remaining with the 18th Cruiser Squadron at Gibraltar for several months.

The early weeks of 1942 saw *Edinburgh* assigned to the protection of convoys sailing the Arctic route to Russia. This was a dangerous task, and it was while she was engaged in this work, on 30 April, that she was hit and disabled by two torpedoes from the *U456* (Lt Cdr Teichert). Despite this, she succeeded in inflicting severe damage on the destroyer *Hermann Schoemann*, one of a force of enemy ships sent out to attack her. One of these ships, however, hit the *Edinburgh* with another torpedo with the result that she had to be abandoned and later sunk by a torpedo from the British destroyer *Foresight* on 2 May 1942.

FORMIDABLE

The Fleet Carrier HMS *Formidable* was one of four laid down in 1937, the others being the *Illustrious, Indomitable* and *Victorious.* All three had armoured flight decks, a feature that was to save them from disaster on several occasions. Launched in August 1939 and completed in November 1940, Formidable was deployed to the Mediterranean in March 1941 and was almost immediately in action, her aircraft achieving torpedo hits on the Italian battleship *Vittorio Veneto* and the cruiser *Pola* at the Battle of Cape Matapan (26–29 March 1941). This was a British victory and somewhat of a triumph for the Fleet Air Arm.

On 26 May 1941 she was badly damaged by German bombs off Crete. She underwent repairs at Norfolk, Virginia, and in 1943 was assigned to the Gibraltar-based Force H. Her aircraft provided cover for the Allied landings on Sicily and in Italy later in the year. In 1944 she was transferred to the Home Fleet, her aircraft taking part in attacks on the German battleship *Tirpitz.*

In 1945 she sailed for the Pacific Ocean and saw action off Okinawa, being twice damaged by *kamikazes* in May near the Japanese hom,e lands. On both occasions, though, her armoured flight deck preserved her from serious harm. Placed in reserve in 1948, she was broken up in 1953.

SPECIFICATIONS

FORMIDABLE

Type: **Fleet Carrier**	*Armour (deck):* **50.8mm (2in)**
Length: **225.55m (740ft)**	*Armour (turrets):* **N/A**
Beam: **28.96m (95ft)**	*Guns:* **16x4.5in**
Draught: **8.54m (28ft)**	*AA guns:* **42x2pdr**
Displacement (normal): **23,957tnes (23,580t)**	*Aircraft:* **36**
Displacement (full load): **29,078tnes (28,620t)**	*Crew:* **1230**
Machinery: **Steam Turbines**	*Launched:* **August 1939**
Armour (belt): **114.3mm (4.5in)**	*Speed:* **32 knots**

FURIOUS

SPECIFICATIONS

FURIOUS

Type: **Fleet Carrier**	Armour (deck): **50.8mm (2in)**
Length: **239.57m (786ft)**	Armour (turrets): **N/A**
Beam: **27.12m (89ft)**	Guns: **10x5.5in; 2x4in**
Draught: **8.23m (27ft)**	AA guns: **4x2pdr**
Displacement (normal): **23,165tnes (22,600t)**	Aircraft: **36**
Displacement (full load): **27,229tnes (26,800t)**	Crew: **1218**
Machinery: **Steam Turbines**	Launched: **August 1916**
Armour (belt): **76.2mm (3in)**	Speed: **31 knots**

Launched in August 1916 and completed in June 1917, HMS *Furious* was laid down as a light battlecruiser, being converted to the role of aircraft carrier by having a hangar and flight deck installed aft. Recommissioned in March 1915, she launched the first successful carrier-borne raid on 19 July 1918, her Sopwith Camel aircraft attacking the German Zeppelin base at Tondern and destroying two airships. Missions such as these proved the viability of aircraft operating from ships, and were a foretaste of things to come in World War II.

In 1921–25 she was fully converted as an aircraft carrier, having a complete flight deck fitted, and in 1939 a small island was added in the course of a refit. During the Norwegian campaign of 1940 she flew off reinforcement aircraft, an exercise successfully repeated in the Mediterranean a year later when she provided reinforcement fighters for Malta on several occasions.

After the German invasion of Russia in June 1941 she operated in Arctic waters, her aircraft attacking German-occupied Norwegian harbour installations, and in 1944 her air group took part in the attacks on the German battleship *Tirpitz*. Her active service over, the veteran carrier was placed in reserve later in the year. She was broken up in 1948.

HERMES

HMS *Hermes* was the first vessel designed from the outset as an aircraft carrier, having a small cruiser-type hull and engines, a full flight deck and large island. Launched on 11 September 1919 and completed in February 1924, she served in the Far East in the years between the two world wars, undergoing a refit in 1933. During her career she was to see much action.

At the outbreak of World War II she was in the South Atlantic, her aircraft being involved in the attack on Dakar in July 1940. She deployed to the East Indies soon afterwards, and in February 1941, on station in the Indian Ocean, she supported the British offensive against the Italians in Somaliland. In the following months she was involved in convoy protection in the Indian Ocean and South Atlantic.

Early in 1942 she was part of the Royal Navy's Eastern Fleet, based at Trincomalee, Ceylon. On 8 April 1942, air reconnaissance reported a Japanese carrier task force approaching the island of Ceylon and *Hermes* was ordered to put to sea, along with the Australian destroyer *Vampire*, the corvette *Hollyhock* and two tankers. The ships were attacked by some 80 Japanese aircraft, and all five were sunk. *Hermes* had no aircraft on board, and was defenceless, her anti-aircraft guns proving ineffective. Over 300 of her crew perished.

SPECIFICATIONS

HERMES

Type: **Fleet Carrier**	*Armour (deck):* **25.4mm (1in)**
Length: **182.88m (600ft)**	*Armour (turrets):* **N/A**
Beam: **21.41m (70.25ft)**	*Guns:* **6x5.5in**
Draught: **6.55m (21.5ft)**	*AA guns:* **3x4in; 6x20mm; 8x.5in**
Displacement (normal): **11,024tnes (10,850t)**	*Aircraft:* **20**
Displacement (full load): **13,208tnes (13,000t)**	*Crew:* **700**
Machinery: **Boilers & Steam Turbines**	*Launched:* **September 1919**
Armour (belt): **76.2mm (3in)**	*Speed:* **25 knots**

HOOD

SPECIFICATIONS

HOOD

Type: **Battlecruiser**	*Armour (deck):* **76.2mm (3in)**
Length: **262.2m (860.5ft)**	*Armour (turrets):* **279.4mm (11in)**
Beam: **32m (105ft)**	*Guns:* **8x15in**
Draught: **10.14m (33.3ft)**	*AA guns:* **14x4in; 24x2pdr; 8x.5in**
Displacement (normal): **42,774tnes (42,100t)**	*Aircraft:* **None**
Displacement (full load): **46,939tnes (46,200t)**	*Crew:* **1421**
Machinery: **Boilers & Steam Turbines**	*Launched:* **August 1918**
Armour (belt): **304.8mm (12in)**	*Speed:* **28.8 knots**

HMS *Hood* was designed as an enlarged version of the "Queen Elizabeth" class battlecruisers in response to the German "Mackensen" class. Launched on 22 August 1918 and completed in March 1920, she was the largest warship in the world, and remained so until World War II. With a speed of 32 knots she was also one of the fastest, deck armour having been sacrificed to produce a higher speed. Much was expected of this vessel in the interwar period.

In 1923–24 she undertook a much-publicized world cruise. Her first operational sortie of World War II was to form part of a blockade across the Iceland-Faeroes-UK gap. In July 1940 she was one of the British ships that bombarded the French harbour of Mers-el-Kebir. In the latter part of 1940 she underwent a refit, during which her spotter aircraft's catapult was removed and her AA armament increased.

In May 1941, together with the battleship *Prince of Wales*, *Hood* sailed to intercept the German battleship *Bismarck* and the heavy cruiser *Prinz Eugen* in the Denmark Strait. In the running battle that followed a salvo from the battleship *Bismarck* plummeted through *Hood*'s lightly-armoured deck and penetrated into a magazine. She blew up at once and sank with the loss of 1338 crew.

INDOMITABLE

A Fleet Carrier of the "Illustrious" class, HMS *Indomitable* was launched on 26 March 1940 and completed in October 1941. In November she went aground off Jamaica while working up, delaying her deployment to the Indian Ocean, where she was to provide the air component of the Eastern Fleet.

In May 1942 she joined her sister ship *Illustrious* in attacking the Vichy French garrison on Madagascar, and in July 1943 she provided air cover for the Sicily invasion force. During these operations she was damaged by an Italian torpedo.

In July 1944 she rejoined the Eastern Fleet, and together with the Royal Navy aircraft carrier *Illustrious*, began a series of attacks on enemy communications in Sumatra. In January 1945, she sailed from Trincomalee for Sydney, Australia, with the carriers *Illustrious*, *Indefatigable* and *Victorious* to form the nucleus of the British Pacific Fleet, and in April saw action off Okinawa, where she, like many ships, was damaged in a *kamikaze* attack. She was again damaged in May, during attacks on the Sakishima-Gunto island group. On her final mission of World War II she led the task force that reoccupied Hong Kong. She underwent a major refit after the war and was placed on the reserve list in 1953, being broken up in 1955.

SPECIFICATIONS

INDOMITABLE

Type: **Fleet Carrier**	*Armour (deck):* **76.2mm (3in)**
Length: **243.84m (800ft)**	*Armour (turrets):* **N/A**
Beam: **28.87m (94.75ft)**	*Guns:* **16x4.5in**
Draught: **8.45m (27.75ft)**	*AA guns:* **16x2pdr; 10x20mm**
Displacement (normal): **22,709tnes (22,352t)**	*Aircraft:* **55**
Displacement (full load): **28,593tnes (28,143t)**	*Crew:* **1600**
Machinery: **Boilers & Steam Turbines**	*Launched:* **March 1940**
Armour (belt): **101.6mm (4in)**	*Speed:* **31 knots**

KELLY

SPECIFICATIONS

KELLY

Type: **Destroyer**	Armour (deck): **12.7mm (.5in)**
Length: **108.66m (356.5ft)**	Armour (turrets): **12.7mm (.5in)**
Beam: **10.87m (35.75ft)**	Guns: **6x4.7in**
Draught: **2.74m (9ft)**	AA guns: **4x2pdr; 8x.5in**
Displacement (normal): **1722tnes (1695t)**	Aircraft: **None**
Displacement (full load): **2367tnes (2330t)**	Crew: **218**
Machinery: **Boilers & Steam Turbines**	Launched: **October 1938**
Armour (belt): **19mm (.75in)**	Speed: **36.5 knots**

Built by Hawthorn Leslie and launched on 25 October 1938, the "K"-class destroyer HMS *Kelly* was destined to become a famous ship with a famous captain – Lord Louis Mountbatten (the exploits of the ship and her captain were made famous in the film *In Which We Serve*, which painted a rather rosy view of life in the wartime Royal Navy). She was active in the closing stages of the Norwegian campaign, covering the evacuation of Allied troops from Namsos and other locations, and on 10 May 1940, during a sortie into the Skagerrak with six other destroyers and the cruiser *Birmingham*, she was badly damaged by a torpedo from the German MTB S31 and had to be towed to Newcastle-upon-Tyne by the destroyer *Bulldog*. After repair she deployed to the Mediterranean, in which all vessels of the "K" and "J" classes served and suffered heavy losses.

Early in May 1941 she was involved in convoy escort duty and also in shelling coastal targets, notably the harbour of Benghazi. The "K" class boats were not particularly well defended against air attack, a deficiency that was to have tragic consequences when Stuka dive-bombers sank both *Kelly* and her sister ship, *Kashmir*, off the island of Crete on 23 May 1941. Of the 17 "K" and "J" class boats that served in the Mediterranean, no fewer than 12 were lost through enemy action.

KING GEORGE V

The five "King George V" class battleships were laid down in 1936–37 as replacements for the Royal Sovereign class of 1913 vintage. Apart from *KGV* herself, the others were *Anson, Duke of York, Howe* and *Prince of Wales*, the latter destined to be sunk off Malaya in December 1941.

King George V was launched on 21 February 1939 and completed on 11 December 1940. Assigned to the Home Fleet, one of her first missions was to transport Prime Minister Churchill to the United States for a meeting with President Roosevelt in January 1941 (one of her sisters also performed this mission – see page 28). In May that year she took part in the hunt for the *Bismarck*, the latter being destroyed by gunfire from the *KGV* and the battleship *Rodney*. *King George V* served in Arctic waters on convoy protection duty and in the Mediterranean, where she was attached to Force H to lend fire support to Allied forces landing on Sicily and at Salerno in 1943.

After a refit in 1944 she sailed to join the British Pacific Fleet. In 1945 she carried out many bombardment missions, some against the Japanese home islands; on one occasion, on 9 July 1945, she put down 267 14in shells on the Hitachi factory near Tokyo. *King George V* was decommissioned in 1949 and broken up in 1958.

SPECIFICATIONS

KING GEORGE V

Type: **Battleship**	*Armour (deck):* **152.6mm (6in)**
Length: **227m (745ft)**	*Armour (turrets):* **330.2mm (13in)**
Beam: **31.39m (103ft)**	*Guns:* **10x14in; 8x5.25in**
Draught: **9.6m (31.5ft)**	*AA guns:* **32x2pdr; 6x20mm**
Displacement (normal): **36,566tnes (35,990t)**	*Aircraft:* **Three**
Displacement (full load): **41,646tnes (40,990t)**	*Crew:* **2000**
Machinery: **Boilers & Steam Turbines**	*Launched:* **February 1939**
Armour (belt): **406.4mm (16in)**	*Speed:* **28.5 knots**

NELSON

SPECIFICATIONS

NELSON

Type: **Battleship**	Armour (deck): **152.4mm (6in)**
Length: **216.4m (710ft)**	Armour (turrets): **406.4mm (16in)**
Beam: **32.3m (106ft)**	Guns: **9x16in; 12x6in**
Draught: **10.79m (35.4ft)**	AA guns: **6x4.7in; 8x2pdr**
Displacement (normal): **36,576tnes (36,000t)**	Aircraft: **None**
Displacement (full load): **43,830tnes (43,140t)**	Crew: **1314**
Machinery: **Boilers & Geared Turbines**	Launched: **September 1925**
Armour (belt): **355.6mm (14in)**	Speed: **23 knots**

HMS *Nelson* and her sister vessel, *Rodney,* were the first British battleships to be constructed after the end of World War I, *Nelson* being launched on 3 September 1925 and completed in June 1927. Her layout was unusual – all her main guns were m,ounted forward. From 1927 to 1941 she was flagship of the Home Fleet, based at Scapa Flow in the Orkneys.

She became an early war casualty, being damaged by a mine off Loch Ewe on 4 September 1939, the day after the outbreak of war, and she did not return to service until August 1940. In the following year she was transferred to the Mediterranean, where she escorted convoys bound for the besieged island of Malta, and on 27 September 1941 she was torpedoed by an Italian aircraft during one such operation, putting her out of action until August 1942.

On 29 September 1943 the armistice agreement with Italy was signed on board her. During the Normandy landings of June 1944 she formed part of the warship force held in reserve for use if necessary by the Western Task Force; and on 12 July she was torpedoed yet again, this time by the German mtor torpedo boat *S138*. After repair at Philadelphia she deployed to the Eastern Fleet, ending her war in the Indian Ocean. She was finally broken up in 1948.

NEWCASTLE

HMS *Newcastle* was one of a class of eight British cruisers, all launched in 1936-37. The others were *Southampton, Birmingham, Glasgow, Sheffield, Liverpool, Manchester* and *Gloucester.* HMS *Newcastle*, originally laid down as *Minotaur*, was the first to be launched, on 23 January 1936.

In 1939–40 she served with the 18th Cruiser Squadron, being based mostly on the river Tyne near her home town. Later in 1940 she deployed to Gibraltar for service in the Mediterranean, and in November took part in the naval engagement with the Italians off Cape Teulada, Sardinia. In 1941 she was engaged in commerce raiding in the South Atlantic, but her main activity during 1941–42 was escorting Mediterranean convoys, providing both defence against enemy naval vessels and ground-based aircraft. This was a highly dangerous mission, especially on the Malta run.

In 1944 she was transferred to the Indian Ocean for convoy protection duties with the Eastern Fleet, her duties also including the escort of aircraft carriers attacking Japanese targets in Sumatra and elsewhere. She was still serving in the Indian Ocean when the war ended. Of the eight ships in this class, three – *Southampton, Manchester* and *Gloucester* – were lost in action in World War II.

SPECIFICATIONS

NEWCASTLE

Type: **Cruiser**	*Armour (deck):* **50.8mm (2in)**
Length: **180.13m (591ft)**	*Armour (turrets):* **25.4mm (1in)**
Beam: **19.5m (64ft)**	*Guns:* **12x6in; 8x4in**
Draught: **6.09m (20ft)**	*AA guns:* **8x2pdr; 8x.5in**
Displacement (normal): **9469tnes (9320t)**	*Aircraft:* **Three**
Displacement (full load): **11,725tnes (11,540t)**	*Crew:* **750**
Machinery: **Steam Turbines**	*Launched:* **January 1936**
Armour (belt): **123.95mm (4.88in)**	*Speed:* **32.5 knots**

QUEEN ELIZABETH

SPECIFICATIONS

QUEEN ELIZABETH

Type: **Dreadnought**	Armour (deck): **63.5mm (2.5in)**
Length: **195.98m (643ft)**	Armour (turrets): **330.2mm (13in)**
Beam: **31.69m (104ft)**	Guns: **8x15in; 4x6in**
Draught: **10.21m (33.5ft)**	AA guns: **2x4in**
Displacement (normal): **29,616tnes (29,150t)**	Aircraft: **None**
Displacement (full load): **33,528tnes (33,000t)**	Crew: **951**
Machinery: **Steam Turbines**	Launched: **October 1913**
Armour (belt): **330.2mm (13in)**	Speed: **25 knots**

The "Queen Elizabeth" class of dreadnoughts, laid down in 1912, also included the *Barham, Malaya, Valiant* and *Warspite*. A sixth vessel, *Agincourt*, was never built. *Queen Elizabeth* was launched on 16 October 1913 and completed in January 1915. She subsequently served on bombardment duty in the ill-starred Dardanelles campaign before rejoining the Grand Fleet, whose flagship she was from 1916 to 1918. However, her anti-aircarft defence was always inadequate

She served in the Mediterranean between the two world wars, undergoing substantial reconstruction in 1926–27 and again in 1937–40. She was recommissioned in January 1941 and based at Alexandria, where in December 1941 she was severely damaged in a daring attack by three Italian "human torpedo" teams, who placed explosive charges under her and her sister ship, HMS *Valiant*. She was made seaworthy and sent to Norfolk, Virginia, for repair, being recommissioned in June 1943. After a spell with the Home Fleet, she was sent to join the Eastern Fleet in the Indian Ocean, where she took part in several bombardment operations against enemy positions in Burma and Sumatra. She was broken up in 1948. She was fortunate to escape the attention of Japanese maritime aircraft, who would have found her an easy prey.

PRINCE OF WALES

Launched on 3 May 1939, the "King George V"-class battleship *Prince of Wales* was the most modern and powerful warship in the Royal Navy when she was completed in March 1941. In fact, she was not fully fitted out when, in May 1941, she was ordered to sea to hunt the German battleship *Bismarck,* and some civilian workmen were still on board. When she came up with *Bismarck* and the heavy cruiser *Prinz Eugen* in the Denmark Strait on 24 May 1941 she received seven hits, compelling her to break off the action. The battlecruiser HMS *Hood* was sunk in this engagement.

In August 1941 the *Prince of Wales* carried Prime Minister Winston Churchill to a meeting with President Roosevelt in Newfoundland; the Atlantic Charter, in which the two Heads of State agreed to co-operate in the defence of their mutual interests, was signed on board her. In December 1941, together with the battlecruiser *Repulse,* the *Prince of Wales* arrived at Singapore, the battleship flying the flag of Admiral Sir Tom Phillips. On 10 December, while searching for a Japanese invasion force, both ships were sunk by enemy bombs and torpedoes, the *Prince of Wales* losing 327 dead, including Admiral Phillips. The attack was proof of the potency of aircraft attack and the eclipse of the battleship as the capital ship of the fleet.

SPECIFICATIONS

PRINCE OF WALES

Type: **Battleship**	*Armour (deck):* **152.4mm (6in)**
Length: **227.07m (745ft)**	*Armour (turrets):* **330.2mm (13in)**
Beam: **31.39m (103ft)**	*Guns:* **10x14in; 8x5.25in**
Draught: **9.6m (31.5ft)**	*AA guns:* **32x2pdr; 16x.5in**
Displacement (normal): **35,565tnes (35,990t)**	*Aircraft:* **Two**
Displacement (full load): **41,646tnes (40,990t)**	*Crew:* **2000**
Machinery: **Steam Turbines**	*Launched:* **March 1941**
Armour (belt): **406.4mm (16in)**	*Speed:* **29 knots**

REPULSE

SPECIFICATIONS

REPULSE

Type: **Battlecruiser**	Armour (deck): **88.9mm (3.5in)**
Length: **242m (794.25ft)**	Armour (turrets): **279.4mm (11in)**
Beam: **27.43m (90ft)**	Guns: **6x15in; 9x4in**
Draught: **9.67m (31.75ft)**	AA guns: **24x2pdr; 16x.5in**
Displacement (normal): **32,512tnes (32,000t)**	Aircraft: **Four**
Displacement (full load): **38,000tnes (37,400t)**	Crew: **1309**
Machinery: **Steam Turbines**	Launched: **August 1916**
Armour (belt): **228.6mm (9in)**	Speed: **32 knots**

Launched and completed in 1916, the battlecruiser HMS *Repulse* served with the Grand Fleet for the rest of World War I but her active career was curtailed by a collision with the battlecruiser *Australia* in December 1917, in which she was damaged. She underwent a refit in 1921–22, in which her armour protection was increased and torpedo tubes added, and in 1923–24 she undertook a world cruise. She was rated as a potent maritime vessel at the time.

She again underwent a refit in 1932–36; on this occasion her superstructure was built up, an aircraft hangar and catapult were added, and her anti-aircraft armament was increased. After this she served in the Mediterranean until 1938, when she rejoined the British Home Fleet.

At the outbreak of World War II *Repulse* joined other British ships in the search for German blockade runners, and in April 1940 she saw action in Norwegian waters. In May 1941 she took part in the search for the *Bismarck*, and later in the year, together with the *Prince of Wales*, she deployed to the Far East to strengthen the defences of Singapore. It was a fatal decision, for on 10 December, while sailing to operate against Japanese forces, both ships were sunk off the east coast of Malaya by Japanese air attack.

RODNEY

One of the Royal Navy's most famous "battlewagons", the "Nelson" class battleship HMS *Rodney* was named after Admiral Lord George Rodney, a celebrated 18th-century British naval commander. She was launched on 17 December 1925 and completed in August 1927.

At the outbreak of World War II she was with the Home Fleet, imposing the blockade of Germany's merchant commerce in northern waters, and she was in action off Norway at the start of the German invasion, being damaged in an air attack.

After repairs and a refit at Boston, Massachusetts, she returned to active service in 1941 in time to take part in the hunt for the *Bismarck*, which her heavy guns helped to destroy; she was later deployed to Gibraltar for escort duty with the Malta convoys. She formed part of the support force during the Allied invasion of North Africa in November 1942, and in the following year supported the Allied landings on Sicily and in southern Italy.

During the D-Day landings in Normandy, June 1944, she was held in reserve to support the Eastern Task Force if required. However, such was the Allied supremacy during the whole invasion operation that her services were not required. She subsequently returned to escort duties, this time in the Arctic. *Rodney* was broken up in 1948.

SPECIFICATIONS

RODNEY

Type: **Battleship**	*Armour (deck):* **152.4mm (6in)**
Length: **216.4m (710ft)**	*Armour (turrets):* **406.4mm (16in)**
Beam: **32.3m (106ft)**	*Guns:* **9x16in; 12x6in**
Draught: **10.76m (35.3ft)**	*AA guns:* **6x4.7in; 8x2pdr**
Displacement (normal): **36,576tnes (36,000t)**	*Aircraft:* **None**
Displacement (full load): **43,830tnes (43,140t)**	*Crew:* **1314**
Machinery: **Steam Turbines**	*Launched:* **December 1925**
Armour (belt): **355.6mm (14in)**	*Speed:* **23 knots**

ROYAL SOVEREIGN

SPECIFICATIONS

ROYAL SOVEREIGN

Type: **Dreadnought**	Armour (deck): **50.8mm (2in)**
Length: **191.19m (624ft)**	Armour (turrets): **330.2mm (13in)**
Beam: **26.97m (88.5ft)**	Guns: **8x15in; 12x6in**
Draught: **8.68m (28.5ft)**	AA guns: **8x4in; 16x2pdr**
Displacement (normal): **28,448tnes (28,000t)**	Aircraft: **One**
Displacement (full load): **31,496tnes (31,000t)**	Crew: **910**
Machinery: **Steam Turbines**	Launched: **April 1915**
Armour (belt): **330.2mm (13in)**	Speed: **21.5 knots**

The "Dreadnought" battleship *Royal Sovereign* was launched on 29 April 1915 and completed in 1916, serving with the Grand Fleet for the duration of World War I. She underwent two refits in the years between the wars, and in 1939–41, in service with the Home Fleet, she was assigned to convoy protection in the Atlantic, also operating in the Mediterranean in 1940. In 1941 she underwent a refit and in 1942, together with four other battleships of World War I vintage, she was assigned to the Eastern Fleet in the Indian Ocean.

On 30 May 1944 she was loaned to the Soviet Union and renamed *Arkhangelsk*. Based in the Arctic, she served as the flagship of Admiral Levchenko and led a powerful escort group whose task was to meet incoming convoys and escort them to the Kola inlet. During this period she saw hard service. On 23 August 1944, for example, while escorting Convoy JW59, she was attacked by the *U711*, whose torpedoes detonated prematurely and thus turned out to be harmless.

In September 1944 the *U315* and *U313* both tried to enter the Kola Inlet to attack her, the attempts being frustrated by net barrages; another attempt in January 1945 by "Biber" midget submarines also failed. *Arkhangelsk* was returned to the Royal Navy in February 1949 and sent to the breaker's yard.

SHEFFIELD

HMS *Sheffield* was a "Southampton"-class cruiser, launched on 23 July 1936 and completed in August 1937. At the outbreak of World War II she was serving in the Home Fleet's 2nd Cruiser Squadron. In April 1940 she acted as a troop transport, carrying men of the 146th Infantry Brigade to Norway, and in August she was sent to Gibraltar to become part of Force H for operations in the Mediterranean. In May 1941 she formed part of the force that was sent out to intercept the *Bismarck*, narrowly avoiding a torpedo attack by British Swordfish aircraft, whose crews mistook her for the massive German battleship!

Reassigned to the Home Fleet, she escorted Arctic convoys to Russia, and in December 1942, she was involved in the Battle of the Barents Sea. This was a notable British victory, during which her gunfire damaged the German heavy cruiser *Admiral Hipper* and sank the destroyer *Friedrich Eckoldt*.

In December 1943, with other Royal Navy cruisers, she engaged the German battlecruiser *Scharnhorst* off North Cape, beginning the action that ended with the *Scharnhorst*'s destruction. She later escorted aircraft carriers carrying out strikes against the *Tirpitz*. *Sheffield* was actively involved in the postwar fleet, and was broken up in 1967.

SPECIFICATIONS

SHEFFIELD

Type: **Cruiser**	Armour (deck): **38.1mm (1.5in)**
Length: **180.29m (591.5ft)**	Armour (turrets): **25.4mm (1in)**
Beam: **18.82m (61.75ft)**	Guns: **12x6in; 8x4in**
Draught: **5.18m (17ft)**	AA guns: **8x2pdr; 8x.5in**
Displacement (normal): **9246tnes (9100t)**	Aircraft: **Two**
Displacement (full load): **11,532tnes (11,350t)**	Crew: **750**
Machinery: **Steam Turbines**	Launched: **August 1937**
Armour (belt): **114.3mm (4.5in)**	Speed: **32 knots**

TRINIDAD

SPECIFICATIONS

TRINIDAD

Type: **Light Cruiser**	Armour (deck): **50.8mm (2in)**
Length: **169.16m (555ft)**	Armour (turrets): **50.8mm (2in)**
Beam: **18.9m (62ft)**	Guns: **12x6in; 8x4in**
Draught: **5.79m (19ft)**	AA guns: **8x2pdr**
Displacement (normal): **9042tnes (8900t)**	Aircraft: **Two**
Displacement (full load): **10,897tnes (10,725t)**	Crew: **730**
Machinery: **Steam Turbines**	Launched: **March 1940**
Armour (belt): **88.9mm (3.5in)**	Speed: **32 knots**

HMS *Trinidad* was one of 11 "Fiji"-class cruisers, and was launched on 21 March 1940, six months after the outbreak of World War II. Her career with the navy was to be interesting.

On 29 March, 1942, while running ahead of an Arctic convoy, she encountered three German destroyers. In a confused engagement in a snowstorm she disabled the destroyer *Z26,* which later sank, but was hit by one of her own torpedoes, which went out of control after being fired to finish off the *Z26.* The submarine *U585* then tried to attack the crippled cruiser, but was sunk by the destroyer *Fury.* The *Trinidad* managed to reach the port of Murmansk, where emergency repairs were made, and on 13 May she set out in company with four destroyers for a point west of Bear Island, where she was to make rendezvous with other British warships. The Russians had promised to provide long-range fighter cover, but only a few aircraft arrived. On the following day *Trinidad* and her escorts were located by enemy air reconnaissance and subjected to torpedo and dive-bomber attacks. One of the latter, delivered by a Junkers Ju 88, hit the *Trinidad* amidships and set her on fire. Bellwoing smoke and badly damaged, the order was given to abandon ship, and *Trinidad* was sunk by the destroyer HMS *Matchless.*

VANGUARD

HMS *Vanguard*, launched on 30 November 1944, was Britain's last battleship and was basically an enlarged "King George V" type, featuring a longer hull to accommodate four twin turrets. Although at this time it was already apparent that she would not be completed before the end of the European war (in fact, she was not completed until April 1946) it was decided to finish her for service in the Pacific, should the war against Japan drag on. Some short cuts were made in her construction, including the installation of the twin 380mm (15in) guns removed from the *Courageous* and *Glorious* when these vessels were converted to aircraft carriers, but many modifications were made as building work progressed and there were inevitable delays.

When she was eventually commissioned she carried the heaviest anti-aircraft armament of any British warship – 71 40mm guns (the lessons that had been learned the hard way by the Royal Navy regarding aerial threats were integrated into this vessel). In 1947 she made headlines when she carried members of the British Royal Family on a state visit to South Africa, and after a refit she served in the Mediterranean in 1949–51, in the training role. After undergoing refits in 1951 and 1954 she was allocated to the reserve in 1956, and was finally broken up in 1960.

SPECIFICATIONS

VANGUARD

Type: **Battleship**	*Armour (deck):* **152.4mm (6in)**
Length: **243.84m (800ft)**	*Armour (turrets):* **381mm (15mm)**
Beam: **32.91m (108ft)**	*Guns:* **8x15in; 16x5.25in**
Draught: **9.22m (30.25ft)**	*AA guns:* **71x40mm**
Displacement (normal): **45,212tnes (44,500t)**	*Aircraft:* **None**
Displacement (full load): **52,243tnes (51,420t)**	*Crew:* **2000**
Machinery: **Steam Turbines**	*Launched:* **November 1944**
Armour (belt): **406.4mm (16in)**	*Speed:* **29.5 knots**

VICTORIOUS

SPECIFICATIONS

VICTORIOUS

Type: **Fleet Carrier**	Armour (deck): **76.2mm (3in)**
Length: **243.84m (800ft)**	Armour (turrets): **N/A**
Beam: **28.88 (94.75ft)**	Guns: **None**
Draught: **8.3m (27.75ft)**	AA guns: **8x4.5in; 16x2pdr**
Displacement (normal): **22,709tnes (22,352t)**	Aircraft: **50**
Displacement (full load): **28,593tnes (28,143t)**	Crew: **900**
Machinery: **Steam Turbines**	Launched: **September 1939**
Armour (belt): **101.6mm (4in)**	Speed: **31 knots**

A Fleet Carrier of the "Illustrious" class, HMS *Victorious* saw action in every theatre of World War II. She and her sisters differed from previous carriers in having an armoured hangar, which reduced the number of aircraft that could be carried but greatly increased the vessels' damage resistance level.

Launched on 14 September 1939 and completed in May 1941, *Victorious* was involved in the hunt for the *Bismarck* only days later. In August 1941 she played a key part in Operation Pedestal, a desperate attempt to run supplies through to Malta, and on several occasions she flew off replacement fighters to the island. In 1942–3 she was assigned to convoy protection duty in the Arctic, and in the following year her air group made a series of attacks on the *Tirpitz*.

In 1944 she deployed to the Indian Ocean, her aircraft attacking Japanese oil refineries at Palembang and Sabang, and in January 1945 she sailed for the Pacific, where she saw considerable action off Okinawa during the desperate Japanese defence of the island. She saw considerable service in the postwar years, being completely reconstructed in 1950–57. In November 1967 she was badly damaged by fire at Portsmouth while refitting, and the decision was finally taken to break her up in 1969.

WARSPITE

A Dreadnought of the "Queen Elizabeth" class, HMS *Warspite* probably saw more action than any other modern British warship and was one of the most important Royal Navy vessels of the war. Launched on 26 November 1913 and completed in March 1915, she fought in the Battle of Jutland in the following year, being severely damaged by 14 hits. *Warspite* was substantially reconstructed between the wars and was in action off Norway in April 1940.

Later in the year she bombarded shore targets in the Mediterranean. In March 1941, during the Battle of Cape Matapan, she and HMS *Valiant* destroyed the Italian cruisers *Zara* and *Fiume*, but in May *Warspite* was severely damaged by enemy aircraft off Crete. Returning to service in 1943, she formed part of the naval forces covering the Allied landings on Sicily and at Salerno, being severely damaged by German air-launched glider bombs during the latter operation. It was decided to effect only partial repairs on her, enabling her to be used in the Allied bombardment force covering the D-Day landings in 1944.

Her active career ended when she was damaged by a mine off Harwich on 13 June. On 23 April 1947, while en route to the breaker's yard, she went aground in Mounts Bay, Cornwall, and was broken up in situ.

SPECIFICATIONS

WARSPITE

Type: **Battleship**	*Armour (deck):* **76.2mm (3in)**
Length: **196.74m (645.5ft)**	*Armour (turrets):* **330.2mm (13in)**
Beam: **31.7m (104ft)**	*Guns:* **8x15in; 12x6in**
Draught: **10.05m (33ft)**	*AA guns:* **8x4.5in; 32x2pdr**
Displacement (normal): **31,816tnes (31,315t)**	*Aircraft:* **Three**
Displacement (full load): **37,037tnes (36450t)**	*Crew:* **1200**
Machinery: **Steam Turbines**	*Launched:* **November 1913**
Armour (belt): **330.2mm (13in)**	*Speed:* **25 knots**

BANDE NERE

SPECIFICATIONS

BANDE NERE

Type: **Light Cruiser**	Armour (deck): **24mm (.95in)**
Length: **169m (554.46ft)**	Armour (turrets): **23mm (.9in)**
Beam: **15.5m (50.85ft)**	Guns: **8x152mm; 6x100mm**
Draught: **5.3m (17.38ft)**	AA guns: **3x37mm; 8x13.2mm**
Displacement (normal): **5283tnes (5200t)**	Aircraft: **None**
Displacement (full load): **7065tnes (6954t)**	Crew: **507**
Machinery: **Turbines**	Launched: **October 1928**
Armour (belt): **20mm (.78in)**	Speed: **37 knots**

The *Bande Nere* – or *Giovanni Delle Bande Nere*, to give the ship her full name – was one of four "Guissano" class light cruisers, laid down for the Italian Navy in 1928. All were destined to be sunk in World War II. They were designed to counter large French destroyers of the "Jaguar", "Lion" and "Aigle" classes.

Bande Nere was launched on 31 October 1928 and completed in April the following year. On 19 July 1940, she and a sister ship, the *Bartolomeo Colleoni*, were engaged by the Australian cruiser *Sydney* and five destroyers in what became known as the Battle of Cape Spada; the *Colleoni* was sunk, 525 of her crew being rescued by the British destroyers, and *Bande Nere* got away after registering a hit on HMAS *Sydney*.

During subsequent operations *Bande Nere* was assigned to the 4th Division, which acted directly under the orders of the Italian Admiralty. Most of the 4th Division's activities involved convoy escort, although it did operate offensively against British Mediterranean convoys. It also undertook some minelaying, mainly in the Sicilian Channel. *Bande Nere* met her end on 1 April 1942, being torpedoed and sunk by the British submarine *Urge* off Stromboli. Though these vessels were fast, they were relatively lightly armed and their anti-aircraft defence was poor.

FIUME

L aunched on 27 April 1930 and completed in
November 1931, *Fiume* was one of four "Zara"– class
heavy cruisers. All four were assigned to the Italian
Navy's 1st Division at the time of Italy's entry into the war
in June 1940.

In March 1941, with her sister cruisers *Zara* and *Pola*
and four destroyers, *Fiume* sailed from Taranto to join
other Italian warships in an attempt to intercept British
convoys heading for Greece. Much was expected by the
Italian High Command, but in the event they were to be
very disappointed. The Italian and British Fleets made
contact on 28 March, and in the ensuing battle, off Cape
Matapan, the battleship *Vittorio Veneto* and the cruiser
Pola were hit by torpedoes in an air attack by aircraft
from the carrier HMS *Formidable*.

The cruisers *Fiume* and *Zara* and the four destroyers
were detached to escort the badly damaged *Pola*, while
the rest of the Italian warships accompanied the *Vittorio
Veneto* to safety. That evening, *Fiume*, *Zara* and *Pole* were
detected by radar equipment on the cruiser HMS *Ajax*
and a few minutes later were engaged by the battleships
Warspite and *Valiant*. They were quickly reduced to
blazing hulks, being finished off by torpedoes. The
crippled *Pola* was also sunk before morning, together
with two of her escorting destroyers.

SPECIFICATIONS

FIUME

Type: **Heavy Cruiser**	*Armour (deck):* **70mm (2.75in)**
Length: **182.8m (600ft)**	*Armour (turrets):* **150mm (5.9in)**
Beam: **20.6m (67.58ft)**	*Guns:* **8x203mm; 16x100mm**
Draught: **7.2m (23.62ft)**	*AA guns:* **4x40mm; 8x12.7mm**
Displacement (normal): **11,685tnes (11,500t)**	*Aircraft:* **None**
Displacement (full load): **14,762tnes (14,530t)**	*Crew:* **841**
Machinery: **Eight Boilers**	*Launched:* **April 1930**
Armour (belt): **70mm (2.75in)**	*Speed:* **27 knots**

GORIZIA

SPECIFICATIONS

GORIZIA

Type: **Heavy Cruiser**	Armour (deck): **70mm (2.75in)**
Length: **182.8m (600ft)**	Armour (turrets): **150m (5.9in)**
Beam: **20.6m (67.58ft)**	Guns: **8x203mm; 16x100mm**
Draught: **7.2m (23.62ft)**	AA guns: **4x40mm; 8x12.7mm**
Displacement (normal): **11,685tnes (11,500t)**	Aircraft: **None**
Displacement (full load): **14,762tnes (14,530t)**	Crew: **841**
Machinery: **Eight Boilers**	Launched: **December 1930**
Armour (belt): **70mm (2.75in)**	Speed: **27 knots**

A sister ship of *Fiume*, *Gorizia* was launched on 28 December 1930 and completed exactly a year later. Unlike her three sisters, which were all destroyed, her operational career lasted until Italy's armistice in September 1943 (when Italy switched sides and joined the Allies). From the outset she was involved in attacks on British convoys, albeit without much success, and after the Battle of Cape Matapan, when the Italian Navy was reorganized, she formed part of the 3rd Division with the heavy cruisers *Trento* and *Trieste*. The principal task of the 3rd Division was convoy protection. She took part in the Second Battle of Sirte, and in June 1942 participated in one of the biggest battles of the Mediterranean war, when German and Italian forces combined to launch a costly attack on two convoys bound for Malta.

On 10 April 1943 she was severely damaged in an attack on Maddalena by B-24 bombers of the US Army Air Force (USAAF), and took no further part in the war. On 8 September 1943, following Italy's armistice with the Allies, *Gorizia* was scuttled at La Maddalena. Raised and refloated by the Germans, she was towed to La Spezia, where she was finally sunk on 26 June 1944 by human torpedoes manned by both British and co-belligerent Italian crews.

LANCIERE

The Italian destroyer *Lanciere* was one of the "Soldati" class, all of which were named after types of soldier (*Lancer, Carabinier, Fusilier* and so on). She was launched on 18 December 1938 and completed on 25 March 1939.

From the start of Italy's war in the Mediterranean she was active in defensive minelaying operations off the Italian coast, serving with the 12th Destroyer Division. Like many Italian warships, she woudl see rough handling at the hands of the Royal Navy. During the sea battle off Cape Teulada (Sardinia) in November 1940, for example, she was badly hit by the cruiser HMS *Berwick* and had to be taken in tow, but she was repaired and in action again early in 1941, escorting Axis convoys to Tripoli in North Africa. This was a dangerous duty, and many merchant vessels were sunk by Allied warships and aircraft.

In September 1941, accompanied by other destroyers of her class, she was once again on minelaying duties, sowing minefields to the southeast of Malta. Her eventual fate was strange. In March 1942 she was one of four destroyers that set out from Messina to escort the cruisers *Bande Nere, Gorizia* and *Trento* en route to the Second Battle of Sirte; in the course of that action on 23 March a severe storm blew up, sinking *Lanciere* and another destroyer, *Scirocco*.

SPECIFICATIONS

LANCIERE

Type: **Destroyer**	*Armour (deck):* **Unknown**
Length: **106m (347.76ft)**	*Armour (turrets):* **Unknown**
Beam: **10.2m (33.46ft)**	*Guns:* **5x120mm**
Draught: **4.35m (14.27ft)**	*AA guns:* **10x20mm**
Displacement (normal): **1859tnes (1830t)**	*Aircraft:* **None**
Displacement (full load): **2500tnes (2460t)**	*Crew:* **187**
Machinery: **Turbines**	*Launched:* **December 1938**
Armour (belt): **Unknown**	*Speed:* **39 knots**

POLA

SPECIFICATIONS

POLA

Type: Heavy Cruiser	**Armour (deck):** 70mm (2.75in)
Length: 182.8m (600ft)	**Armour (turrets):** 150mm (5.9in)
Beam: 20.6m (67.58ft)	**Guns:** 8x203mm; 16x100mm
Draught: 7.2m (23.62ft)	**AA guns:** 4x40mm; 8x12.7mm
Displacement (normal): 11,685tnes (11,500t)	**Aircraft:** None
Displacement (full load): 14,762tnes (14,530t)	**Crew:** 841
Machinery: Boilers	**Launched:** December 1931
Armour (belt): 70mm (2.75in)	**Speed:** 27 knots

The "Zara"-class heavy cruiser *Pola* was launched on 5 December 1931 and completed on 21 December the following year. On Italy's entry into World War II she was assigned to the 3rd Cruiser Division at Messina, together with the *Trento* and *Bolzano*.

In the early naval actions in the Mediterranean, when the Italians had at least some parity with the Royal Navy, she was the flagship of Admiral Paladini. Later in 1940 she was assigned to the 1st Division, and in October she was involved in attempts to intercept heavy units of the Royal Navy heading for Malta with troop reinforcements.

During the battle of Cape Teulada in November 1940 she managed to out-manoeuvre determined attacks by torpedo aircraft from the *Ark Royal*. On 14 December she was damaged in a British air attack on Naples, but repairs were effected in time to sail to take part in the Battle of Cape Matapan. It was to prove a disaster for the Italian Navy, for unknown to its High Command the British were aware of the Italian Fleet's movements through "Ultra" intelligence intercepts. In the night of 28-29 1941 March *Pola* was hit by a torpedo in the course of an air attack and disabled. Further damaged by British gunfire, she was fatally damaged and thus abandoned by her crew. Her hull was finished off by several British destroyers.

VITTORIO VENETO

The Italian battleship *Vittorio Veneto*, whose name commemorated the Italian Army's victory over the Austrians on 3 November 1918, was launched on 22 July 1937 and completed in April 1940. She was one of th emost powerful vessels in the Italians Navy, and much was expected of her.

She narrowly missed being damaged in the Fleet Air Arm torpedo attack on Taranto in November 1940, and again when she put to sea later in the month. In the Battle of Cape Matapan, March 1941, she was attacked by torpedo-carrying Swordfish aircraft from the carrier HMS *Formidable*. Three torpedoes were dropped at close range and one of them struck her just above her port outer propeller, quickly flooding her with thousands of tons of water.

The Italian commander, Admiral Iachino (the *Veneto* was his flagship), broke off the action and units of his fleet escorted the battleship to safety. On 14 December 1941 she was torpedoed by the British submarine *Urge* while escorting a convoy to Libya, and in June she was further damaged in a US air attack on *La Spezia*. The *Veneto* surrendered to the Allies in September 1943 and was interned in the Suez Canal until 1946. It took several years to strip her down, and she was finally broken up at La Spezia in 1960.

SPECIFICATIONS

VITTORIO VENETO

Type: **Battleship**	*Armour (deck):* **10mm (.39in)**
Length: **237.8m (780ft)**	*Armour (turrets):* **350mm (13.79in)**
Beam: **32.9m (107.93ft)**	*Guns:* **9x12in; 12x6in; 12x90mm**
Draught: **10.5m (34.49ft)**	*AA guns:* **20x37mm**
Displacement (normal): **41,167tnes (40,517t)**	*Aircraft:* **Three**
Displacement (full load): **46,484tnes (45,752t)**	*Crew:* **1920**
Machinery: **Boilers**	*Launched:* **July 1937**
Armour (belt): **350mm (13.79in)**	*Speed:* **30 knots**

ZARA

SPECIFICATIONS

ZARA

Type: **Heavy Cruiser**	Armour (deck): **70mm (2.75in)**
Length: **182.8m (600ft)**	Armour (turrets): **150mm (5.9in)**
Beam: **20.6m (67.58ft)**	Guns: **8x203mm; 16x100mm**
Draught: **7.2m (23.62ft)**	AA guns: **4x40mm; 8x12.7mm**
Displacement (normal): **11,685tnes (11,500t)**	Aircraft: **None**
Displacement (full load): **14,762tnes (14,530t)**	Crew: **841**
Machinery: **Boilers**	Launched: **April 1930**
Armour (belt): **70mm (2.75in)**	Speed: **33 knots**

*Z*ara was class leader of a group of four heavy cruisers, the others being *Fiume*, *Gorizia* and *Pola*. She was launched on 27 April 1930, completed on 20 October 1931, and her operational career almost exactly matched that of her sister ships *Fiume* and *Pola*, all three vessels being sunk by the British at the Battle of Cape Matapan in March 1941.

The "Zara" class ships, originally classed at light cruisers, then armoured cruisers and finally heavy cruisers, were intended to be an improvement on the earlier "Trento" class, completed in the 1920s. However, the experiment was not a success. It was soon realised that the intended increase in armour protection, speed and gunnery could not be provided under the 10,160-tonne (10,000-ton) limit imposed by the various naval treaties between the wars, although when completed the displacement of the vessels exceeded the treaty limit by 1524 tonnes (1500 tons).

All four ships were equipped with a launch catapult and a hangar capable of accommodating two spotter aircraft was fitted beneath the forecastle. Although the ships were capable of over 33 knots, higher speed was sacrificed for greater armour protection; in fact, the weight of armour installed was three times that of the "Trento" class.

AKAGI

*A*kagi, named after a mountain northwest of Tokyo, was originally laid down as a high-speed battlecruiser, one of a class of four. The other three (*Amagi, Atago* and *Takao)* were cancelled in 1922 because of the restrictions imposed by the Washington Naval Treaty and construction of *Akagi* was suspended when she was 40 per cent complete, but in 1923 it was decided to re-order *Akagi* as an aircraft carrier. The decision was a good one with regard to the type of war the navy would fight in the Pacific Ocean.

She was launched in her new guise on 22 April 1925 and completed in March 1927. In her original aircraft carrier configuration she had three flight decks forward, no island and two funnels on the starboard side, but during substantial reconstruction in 1935–38 the two lower flight decks forward were removed and the top flight deck extended forward to the bow. An island was also added on the port side.

In December 1941 *Akagi* was part of the carrier task force that attacked Pearl Harbor; in subsequent operations her aircraft also attacked targets on Rabaul, Java and Ceylon and took part in raids on Darwin early in 1942. On 4 June 1942 *Akagi* was severely damaged by US aircraft at the Battle of Midway and had to be sunk by the destroyers *Nowake* and *Arashi*.

SPECIFICATIONS

AKAGI

Type: **Aircraft Carrier**	*Armour (deck):* **76.2mm (3in)**
Length: **261m (856ft)**	*Armour (turrets):* **N/A**
Beam: **31.4m (103ft)**	*Guns:* **6x102mm; 12x127mm**
Draught: **8.7m (28.54ft)**	*AA guns:* **28x25mm**
Displacement (normal): **37,084tnes (36,500t)**	*Aircraft:* **91**
Displacement (full load): **41,961tnes (41,300t)**	*Crew:* **2000**
Machinery: **Steam Turbines**	*Launched:* **April 1925**
Armour (belt): **152.4mm (6in)**	*Speed:* **31.5 knots**

HARUNA

SPECIFICATIONS

HARUNA

Type:
Battlecruiser

Armour (deck):
55.88mm (2.2in)

Length:
215m (704ft)

Armour (turrets):
228.6mm (9in)

Beam:
28.04m (92ft)

Guns:
8x14in; 16x6in; 8x3in

Draught:
8.38m (27.5ft)

AA guns:
None

Displacement (normal):
27,940tnes (27,500t)

Aircraft:
Three

Displacement (full load):
32,817tnes (32,300t)

Crew:
1221

Machinery:
Steam Turbines

Launched:
December 1913

Armour (belt):
203.2mm (8in)

Speed:
27 knots

The battlecruiser *Haruna* and her three sisters, *Hiei, Kirishima* and *Kongo*, were designed by an Englishman, Sir George Thurston, and embodied some improvements based on experience with the British "Lion" class. *Haruna* was launched on 14 December 1913 and completed in April 1915. All four ships underwent two periods of extensive reconstruction between the wars, after which they were reclassified as battleships. A major problem with all the ships was the lack of proper anti-aircraft defences.

In December 1941 she formed part of the naval force covering the Japanese landings in Malaya and the East Indies, and escorted the aircraft carriers whose aircraft carried out a major attack on Darwin in February 1942 and on Ceylon in April.

In June 1942 she took part in the Battle of Midway, and later on she participated in the Battles of Guadalcanal, Santa Cruz, Philippine Sea and Leyte Gulf. During the Battle of the Philippine Sea, she was damaged by air attack on 19 June 1944. On 18 March 1945 she was again damaged by air attack while at anchor off Kure, and on 28 July she was sunk by US carrier aircraft at that same location. She was refloated and broken up at Harima in 1946. The name *Haruna* derives from a mountain in north central Honshu.

HIEI

A sister ship of *Haruna*, the battlecruiser *Hiei* – reclassified as a battleship after reconstruction in the 1930s – was launched on 21 November 1912 and completed on 4 August 1914. A few weeks later she took part in the search for the German Admiral von Spee's South Atlantic Squadron, which was eventually destroyed by the Royal Navy off the Falkland Islands. Between periods of reconstruction *Hiei* – which was demilitarized under the terms of the London Naval Treaty of 1922 – was used as a cadet training ship. During World War II she performed well enough when the Japanese had aerial supremacy, but was very vulnerable when this was not the case.

Fully modernized by 1941, she formed part of the Japanese task force whose carrier aircraft attacked Pearl Harbor, and subsequently saw action during the invasion of the East Indies – when she and the *Kirishima* sank the US destroyer *Edsall* south of Java – the attack on Ceylon, and the Battles of Midway, the Eastern Solomons, Santa Cruz and Guadalcanal. During the latter operation, in what became known as the First Battle of Guadalcanal, she was sunk by American gunfire, torpedoes and air attack off Savo Island on 13 November 1942. This action took place at night, the US warships involved having the major advantage of radar.

SPECIFICATIONS

HIEI

Type: **Battlecruiser**	*Armour (deck):* **55.88mm (2.2in)**
Length: **214.57m (704ft)**	*Armour (turrets):* **228.6mm (9in)**
Beam: **28.04m (92ft)**	*Guns:* **8x14in; 16x6in; 8x3in**
Draught: **8.38m (27.5ft)**	*AA guns:* **None**
Displacement (normal): **27,940tnes (27,500t)**	*Aircraft:* **Three**
Displacement (full load): **32,817tnes (32,300t)**	*Crew:* **1201**
Machinery: **Boilers & Steam Turbines**	*Launched:* **November 1912**
Armour (belt): **203.2mm (8in)**	*Speed:* **27 knots**

HOSHO

SPECIFICATIONS

HOSHO

Type: **Aircraft Carrier**	Armour (deck): **None**
Length: **248m (813.64ft)**	Armour (turrets): **N/A**
Beam: **32.6m (107ft)**	Guns: **4x140mm**
Draught: **9.5m (31.17ft)**	AA guns: **8x25mm**
Displacement (normal): **7590tnes (7470t)**	Aircraft: **21**
Displacement (full load): **9785tnes (9630t)**	Crew: **550**
Machinery: **Steam Turbines**	Launched: **November 1921**
Armour (belt): **None**	Speed: **25 knots**

Originally projected in 1919 as an auxiliary tanker capable of carrying aircraft, *Hosho*, whose name means "Soaring Phoenix", was in fact completed as Japan's first dedicated aircraft carrier, being launched on 13 November 1921 and completed in December 1922. Built with British assistance, she was extensively used for trials and development work. She had a small bridge and three funnels, which could be swung down during flying operations; the bridge was removed in 1923 and the flight deck made flush to improve aircraft operation. *Hosho* was also fitted with a system of mirrors and lights to assist pilots in landing. It was by such measures and training that the Japanese naval pilots were among the best in the world when war broke out in 1941.

During the Sino-Japanese war *Hosho*'s air group was used to provide close air support; she was afterwards relegated to the training role, but became operational again on Japan's entry into World War II and saw active service during the Battle of Midway before reverting to training duties. On 19 March 1945 she was damaged in an air attack on the naval base at Kure (her antiaircraft defences were totally inadequate at this time), and was disarmed on 20 April. At the war's end she was used to repatriate prisoners of war, and was broken up at Osaka in April 1947.

HYUGA

A Dreadnought of the "Ise" class, *Hyuga*, named after a province of southeast Kyushu, was launched on 27 January 1917 and completed in April 1918. In 1934–36, in common with other capital ships of the Imperial Japanese Navy, she underwent a complete reconstruction, improvements including thicker deck armour and the addition of anti-torpedo bulges.

In June 1942 she formed part of the escort force whose carriers launched their aircraft at the island of Midway. As a result of the staggering carrier losses sustained by the Japanese in this battle, *Hyuga* and others of her class were converted as "battleship-carriers" in 1943, being fitted with a hangar which could house 22 seaplanes. The idea was that all the aircraft would be catapult-launched in 20 minutes, alighting on the sea on their return and being hoisted aboard by cranes. The scheme was not tested in combat because of a critical shortage of both aircraft and pilots (by this stage of the war the Americans had such a superiority in carriers and aircraft that it would have made little difference).

Hyuga was in action during the Battle of Leyte Gulf, where she formed part of a decoy force. She was deactivated on 1 March 1945 and sunk in shallow water near Kure by US aircraft on 24 July. *Hyuga* was refloated and broken up in 1952.

SPECIFICATIONS

HYUGA

Type: **Dreadnought**	*Armour (deck):* **76.2mm (3in)**
Length: **205.74m (675ft)**	*Armour (turrets):* **304.8mm (12in)**
Beam: **28.65m (94ft)**	*Guns:* **12x14in; 20x5.5in; 4x3in**
Draught: **8.83m (29ft)**	*AA guns:* **None**
Displacement (normal): **31,760tnes (31,260t)**	*Aircraft:* **None**
Displacement (full load): **37,084tnes (36,500t)**	*Crew:* **1360**
Machinery: **Boilers & Steam Turbines**	*Launched:* **January 1917**
Armour (belt): **304.8mm (12in)**	*Speed:* **23 knots**

KAGA

SPECIFICATIONS

KAGA

Type: **Aircraft Carrier**	Armour (deck): **58.42mm (2.3in)**
Length: **240.48m (789ft)**	Armour (turrets): **N/A**
Beam: **32.91m (108ft)**	Guns: **None**
Draught: **9.44m (31ft)**	AA guns: **25x20mm; 30x13.2mm**
Displacement (normal): **26,417tnes (26,000t)**	Aircraft: **85**
Displacement (full load): **34,233tnes (33,693t)**	Crew: **1340**
Machinery: **Boilers & Steam Turbines**	Launched: **November 1920**
Armour (belt): **279.4mm (11in)**	Speed: **27.5 knots**

*K*aga was laid down as a battleship and launched on 17 November 1920. Under the terms of the 1921 Washington Treaty she was to have been scrapped, but instead the Imperial Japanese Navy decided to complete her as an aircraft carrier to replace another carrier, the *Amagi*, which had been destroyed in an earthquake while under construction. She was completed in March 1928 and joined the Combined Fleet in 1930. In 1934–35 she was reconstructed, a full-length flight deck and island being added. This made her one of the major aircraft carriers in the navy at the beginning of the war in December 1941.

Recommissioned in June 1935, she was assigned to the First Carrier Division with the *Akagi*, her air group seeing action during the Sino-Japanese war. Her career during World War II was short but spectacular.

In December 1941 her aircraft attacked Pearl Harbour, and subsequently operated over Rabaul, Darwin and Java. She then formed part of the Japanese carrier task force assembled for the assault on Midway Island. Concentrating on the destruction of Midway's air defences, the Japanese carriers were caught unprepared when American dive-bombers and torpedo-bombers launched their counter-attack; *Akagi*, *Kaga* and *Soryu* were all sunk, *Kaga* suffering 800 dead.

KIRISHIMA

The "Kongo"-class battlecruiser *Kirishima* (named after a mountain in Kyushu) was launched on 1 December 1913 and completed in April 1915. In the 1930s, like others of her kind, she underwent major reconstruction and was reclassified as a battleship in preparation for the war in the Pacific Ocean. As well as having a formidable main armament, she was well equipped with antiaircraft guns.

In December 1941 she was assigned to escort the carriers whose aircraft attacked Pearl Harbor; she subsequently covered the Japanese landings at Rabaul and in the Dutch East Indies, and on 1 March 1942 she assisted in the sinking of the destroyer USS *Edsall* south of Java. In the months that followed she participated in almost all Japanese naval actions in the South Pacific. During the naval battles near the Santa Cruz islands, preceding the assault on Guadalcanal, she bore an apparently charmed life; on 25 October 1942 she experienced several near misses when Boeing B-17s bombed her and she was attacked by torpedo-armed aircraft. In November she bombarded Henderson Field on Guadalcanal in support of a Japanese invasion force. Her luck finally ran out on 15 November 1942, though, when she was sunk by the gunfire of the US battleship *Washington*.

SPECIFICATIONS

KIRISHIMA

Type: **Battlecruiser**	Armour (deck): **55.88mm (2.2in)**
Length: **214.67m (704ft)**	Armour (turrets): **228.6mm (9in)**
Beam: **28.04m (92ft)**	Guns: **8x14in; 16x6in; 8x3in**
Draught: **8.38m (27.5ft)**	AA guns: **4x40mm; 8x13.2mm**
Displacement (normal): **27,940tnes (27,500t)**	Aircraft: **Three**
Displacement (full load): **32,817tnes (32,300t)**	Crew: **1221**
Machinery: **Boilers & Steam Turbines**	Launched: **December 1913**
Armour (belt): **203.2mm (8in)**	Speed: **27 knots**

KONGO

SPECIFICATIONS

KONGO

Type: **Battlecruiser**	Armour (deck): **55.88mm (2.2in)**
Length: **214.57m (704ft)**	Armour (turrets): **228.6mm (9in)**
Beam: **28.04m (92ft)**	Guns: **8x14in; 16x6in; 8x3in**
Draught: **8.38m (27.5ft)**	AA guns: **4x40mm; 8x13.2mm**
Displacement (normal): **27,940tnes (27,500t)**	Aircraft: **Three**
Displacement (full load): **32,817tnes (32,300t)**	Crew: **1201**
Machinery: **Steam Turbines**	Launched: **May 1912**
Armour (belt): **203.2mm (8in)**	Speed: **27 knots**

The battlecruiser *Kongo* was built by the British firm Vickers-Armstrong at Barrow-in-Furness, England, and was the first ship in the Imperial Japanese Navy to be fitted with 355mm (14in) guns (her construction shows the good relationships between the British and the Japanese at this period). She was launched on 18 May 1912 and completed in August 1913. In the early weeks of World War I she took part in the search for Admiral von Spee's South Atlantic Squadron, which destroyed a British naval force at Coronel before being itself destroyed off the Falkland Islands.

Between the two world wars *Kongo* underwent two periods of reconstruction, after which she was reclassed as a high-speed battleship. After the outbreak of the Pacific war she was an active member of the fleet: she covered the Japanese landings in Malaya, formed part of the force escorting the aircraft carriers whose aircraft attacked Darwin and Ceylon, and in June 1942, as part of the 3rd Battleship Squadron, she formed a key escort element of the force that was to have invaded Midway Island. She featured in the battles of Guadalcanal, Santa Cruz, the Philippine Sea and Leyte Gulf, and on 21 November 1944 she was torpedoed and sunk by the submarine USS *Sealion* some 105km (65 miles) northwest of Keelung.

MOGAMI

The four ships of the "Mogami" light cruiser class were designed to mount the heaviest possible armament on the restricted tonnage set by the London Naval Treaty of 1930. They featured triple gun turrets and, following the example of Germany's "pocket battleships", their hulls were electrically welded to save weight. During trials, however, they proved to be unstable, and the first two ships – *Mogami* and *Mikuma* – were taken out of service for alterations.

Launched on 14 March 1934, *Mogami* and *Mikuma* both took part in the Battle of Midway in June 1942, the former being sunk and the latter severely damaged by carrier aircraft from the USS *Yorktown*. After repairs *Mogami* was returned to service in 1943, having been fitted with a flight deck on which it was intended to carry 11 seaplanes (as part of the Japanese's desperate attempt to augment their naval air power following severe losses). The cruiser was again damaged in action off the Solomons in July 1943; repaired a second time, she was back in service with the 7th Cruiser Squadron in 1944. On 25 October she was sunk by air attack at the Battle of the Surigao Strait. None of the other ships of the "Mogami" class survived the war; *Suzuya* was lost at the Battle of Leyte Gulf and *Kumano* was sunk by US aircraft in Colon Bay.

SPECIFICATIONS

MOGAMI

Type: **Cruiser**	*Armour (deck):* **38mm (1.5in)**
Length: **200m (656.16ft)**	*Armour (turrets):* **127mm (5in)**
Beam: **20.5m (65.61ft)**	*Guns:* **15x155mm; 8x127mm**
Draught: **10.9m (35.76ft)**	*AA guns:* **8x25mm**
Displacement (normal): **12,599tnes (12,400t)**	*Aircraft:* **Three**
Displacement (full load): **13,188tnes (12,980t)**	*Crew:* **930**
Machinery: **Geared Turbines**	*Launched:* **March 1934**
Armour (belt): **100mm (3.93in)**	*Speed:* **36 knots**

MUTSU

SPECIFICATIONS

MUTSU

Type: **Battleship**	Armour (deck): **76.2mm (3in)**
Length: **213.36m (700ft)**	Armour (turrets): **355.6mm (14in)**
Beam: **28.95m (95ft)**	Guns: **8x16in; 20x5.5in; 4x3in**
Draught: **9.14m (30ft)**	AA guns: **20x25mm**
Displacement (normal): **34,431tnes (33,800t)**	Aircraft: **Three**
Displacement (full load): **39,116tnes (38,500t)**	Crew: **1333**
Machinery: **Steam Turbines**	Launched: **May 1920**
Armour (belt): **304.8mm (12in)**	Speed: **25 knots**

Launched on 31 May 1920 and completed in October 1921, the "Dreadnought" battleship *Mutsu* (an ancient name for the provinces of northern Honshu) was the second warship of the "Nagato" class. She was extensively modified in two refits between the wars. In 1934–36, based at Yokosuka, she was used for long-range reconnaissance in the Pacific, gathering much information which was of great value when the Imperial Japanese Navy went to war five years later (though the activities of such a large ship seem to have totally eluded the Americans).

In June 1942, at the Battle of Midway, she was part of the Midway Support Group, which came under the direct orders of Admiral Yamamoto and also included the battleships *Nagato* and *Yamato*. In July 1942, following the abortive Midway operation, *Mutsu* was assigned to the 2nd Battleship Squadron of the First Fleet under Vice-Admiral Takasu, together with the battleships *Nagato*, *Fuso* and *Yamashiro*.

In August 1942, during the battle off the Solomon Islands that preceded the Japanese landings on Guadalcanal, she led a support group that included the seaplane carrier *Chitose*. On 8 June 1942, while at anchor in Hiroshima Bay, *Mutsu* was destroyed by an internal magazine explosion with the loss of 1222 lives.

MYOKO

*M*yoko was the leader of a class of 10,160-tonne (10,000-ton) cruisers, the others being *Ashigara*, *Haguro* and *Nachi*. She was launched on 16 April 1927. As with other cruiser classes of this period, the "Myokos", thanks to advanced design and shipbuilding techniques, mounted the maximum armament and achieved the highest possible speeds while conforming to the tonnage restrictions of the Washington Treaty. They were useful vessels, and would prove their worth during the campaign in the Pacific, though they all suffered at the hands of the Alllies.

During World War II the ships of this class formed the Fifth Cruiser Division. In December 1941 they participated in the Japanese landings in the Philippines, and all their subsequent operations were conducted in the area of the Dutch East Indies, Malaya. and the Philippines. On 24 October 1944, during Allied operations to recapture the Philippines, *Myoko* was torpedoed by an American aircraft and deemed to be a constructive total loss on 13 December.

Of the other ships in the class, *Nachi* was sunk by US air attack in Manila Bay in November 1944; *Haguro* was sunk by British destroyers off Penang in May 1945; and *Ashigara* was sunk in June 1945 in the Bangka Strait, Indonesia, by the British submarine *Trenchant*.

SPECIFICATIONS

MYOKO

Type: Cruiser	**Armour (deck):** 127mm (5in)
Length: 207m (679.13ft)	**Armour (turrets):** 76.2mm (3in)
Beam: 19m (62.33ft)	**Guns:** 10x203mm; 6x120mm
Draught: 6.3m (20.75ft)	**AA guns:** 8x25mm
Displacement (normal): 12,568tnes (12,370t)	**Aircraft:** Two
Displacement (full load): 13,594tnes (13,380t)	**Crew:** 792
Machinery: Geared Turbines	**Launched:** April 1927
Armour (belt): 102mm (4.01in)	**Speed:** 33 knots

NAGATO

SPECIFICATIONS

NAGATO

Type:
Battleship

Length:
213.36m (700ft)

Beam:
28.95m (95ft)

Draught:
9.14m (30ft)

Displacement (normal):
34,341tnes (33,800t)

Displacement (full load):
39,116tnes (38,500t)

Machinery:
Steam Turbines

Armour (belt):
304.8mm (12in)

Armour (deck):
76.2mm (3in)

Armour (turrets):
355.6mm (14in)

Guns:
8x16in; 20x5.5in

AA guns:
20x25mm

Aircraft:
Three

Crew:
1333

Launched:
November 1919

Speed:
27 knots

The two ships of the "Nagato" class (the other was the *Mutsu*) were laid down in the closing stages of World War one as part of the Japanese Navy's so-called "8-8" programme, which envisaged the building of eight battleships and eight battlecruisers. Launched on 9 November 1919, *Nagato* was completed in November 1920.

During substantial reconstruction work at Kure in 1934–36, her fore funnel was removed, she was re-engined and re-boilered, anti-torpedo bulges were added, the elevation of her main armament was increased to give the guns a better anti-aircraft capability (though using main guns to shoot down aircraft appears to have been a desperate measure), and a clipper bow was fitted. During the early months of the Pacific War she was flagship of the Imperial Japanese Combined Fleet, and as such she saw action at Midway and in the Battle of the Philippine Sea.

In October 1944, during the Battle of Leyte Gulf, she was damaged by aircraft bombs at Samar. She took no further part in the war, being laid up at Yokosuka, and surrendered to the Allies there in September 1945. In July 1946 she was used as a target ship for the US nuclear tests at Bikini; severely damaged in the second test, she sank on 29 July.

ZUIKAKU

The Fleet Carriers *Zuikaku* ("Lucky Crane") and *Shokaku* ("Happy Crane") were both laid down after the expiry of the Naval Treaties of the 1930s, and consequently no limitations were placed on their design. They had strengthened flight decks, a very long range, and were capable of 34 knots. However, armament against aerial attack was rather neglected, which would prove fata.

The vessels formed part the 5th Carrier Squadron of Admiral Nagumo's 1st Naval Air Fleet, and took part in the attack on Pearl Harbor on 7 December 1941. *Zuikaku* subsequently took part in every Japanese naval action of the Pacific war up to and including the Battle of Leyte Gulf, with the exception of the Battle of Midway; her absence, and that of *Shokaku*, was due to a shortage of maritime aviation pilots and to substantial damage sustained in the Battle of the Coral Sea, where *Shokaku* received three bombs hits. *Shokaku* was sunk by three torpedoes from the US submarine *Cavalla* on 19 June 1944, during the Battle of the Philippine Sea; *Zuikaku* survived a little longer to take part in the Battle of Leyte Gulf, but on 25 October 1944 she was sunk in a massive attack by 326 American dive-bombers and torpedo aircraft, which also destroyed the carriers *Chitose*, *Zuiho* and *Chiyoda*.

SPECIFICATIONS

ZUIKAKU

Type: **Aircraft Carrier**	*Armour (deck):* **129.54mm (5.1in)**
Length: **257.5m (844.81ft)**	*Armour (turrets):* **N/A**
Beam: **28m (91.86ft)**	*Guns:* **16x127mm**
Draught: **8.9m (29.19ft)**	*AA guns:* **36x25mm**
Displacement (normal): **26,086tnes (25,675t)**	*Aircraft:* **84**
Displacement (full load): **32,618tnes (32,105t)**	*Crew:* **1660**
Machinery: **Steam Turbines**	*Launched:* **November 1939**
Armour (belt): **165.1mm (6.5in)**	*Speed:* **34.2 knots**

ALABAMA

SPECIFICATIONS

ALABAMA

Type: **Battleship**	Armour (deck): **38.1mm (1.5in)**
Length: **207.26m (680ft)**	Armour (turrets): **457.2mm (18in)**
Beam: **32.91m (108ft)**	Guns: **9x16in; 36x5in**
Draught: **8.91m (29.25ft)**	AA guns: **28x1.1in; 24x40mm**
Displacement (normal): **35,966tnes (35,400t)**	Aircraft: **Three**
Displacement (full load): **45,923tnes (45,200t)**	Crew: **1793**
Machinery: **Steam Turbines**	Launched: **February 1942**
Armour (belt): **309.88mm (12.2in)**	Speed: **27 knots**

The fourth and last battleship of the "South Dakota" class, the USS *Alabama* (BB60) was launched on 16 February 1942 and completed in August of that year. After a period of working up and convoy protection duty in the Arctic, she and the *South Dakota* arrived at Scapa Flow in June 1943, releasing two British battleships for service in the Mediterranean to cover the Allied landings on Sicily.

The two American battleships then transferred to the Pacific, forming part of Task Group 58.2, and in January 1944 they took part in attacks on Japanese bases in the Marshall Islands. *Alabama* subsequently participated in all the US Navy's main fleet actions in the Pacific, being involved in the Battle of the Philippine Sea and in actions at the Gilbert Islands, Truk, Palau, Saipan, Guam, Luzon, Taiwan, Okinawa and the bombardment of the Japanese home islands. It was a role to which the big battleships were ideally suited, especially as the Americans had almost total supremacy in the air and could give the ships protection.

On 5 June 1945 she was damaged in a typhoon off Okinawa. She was decommissioned in January 1947, but was not stricken until June 1962. She was subsequently transferred to the State of Alabama, to be preserved as a permanent memorial at the naval base of Mobile.

ATLANTA

Launched on 6 September 1941, the USS *Atlanta* was the leader of a class of 11 light anti-aircraft cruisers (the Americans had seen the dangers that enemy aircraft posed to their maritime vessels and fleets). In June 1942 she was in action at the Battle of Midway, and in August she was one of the warships covering the American landing in the island of Guadalcanal, later taking part in the sea and air battle that raged east of the Solomons as US and Japanese forces battled for possession of that strategic position.

In October 1942, as one of the cruisers providing the anti-aircraft screen for Task Force 64, she was present at the Battle of Santa Cruz, and later provided escort to the convoys carrying vital supplies to the US forces on Guadalcanal. On 6 November 1942 she sailed from Espiritu Santu as part of Task Group 62.4, escorting a troop convoy bound for the island. The convoy arrived on the 12th and began the process of disembarking, but this was halted when air reconnaissance reported strong Japanese naval forces approaching. In a series of fierce night engagements the American force was broken up, the *Atlanta* sinking in the early hours of 13 November after receiving gun and torpedo hits. The name *Atlanta* was later assumed by a cruiser of the "Cleveland-Fargo" class, launched in June 1944.

SPECIFICATIONS

ATLANTA

Type: **Antiaircraft Cruiser**	Armour (deck): **30.48mm (1.2in)**
Length: **165.5m (543ft)**	Armour (turrets): **30.48mm (1.2in)**
Beam: **16.55m (54.3ft)**	Guns: **16x5in**
Draught: **6.09m (20ft)**	AA guns: **3x1.1in; 24x40 & 14x20m**
Displacement (normal): **6096tnes (6000t)**	Aircraft: **None**
Displacement (full load): **2591tnes (8500t)**	Crew: **590**
Machinery: **Steam Turbines**	Launched: **September 1941**
Armour (belt): **88.9mm (3.5in)**	Speed: **32.5 knots**

AUGUSTA

SPECIFICATIONS

AUGUSTA

Type: **Heavy Cruiser**	*Armour (deck):* **76.2mm (3in)**
Length: **182.88m (600ft)**	*Armour (turrets):* **38.1mm (1.5in)**
Beam: **20.91m (66.25ft)**	*Guns:* **9x8in; 8x5in**
Draught: **7.01m (23ft)**	*AA guns:* **32x40mm; 27x20mm**
Displacement (normal): **9195tnes (9050t)**	*Aircraft:* **Four**
Displacement (full load): **12,497tnes (12,300t)**	*Crew:* **872**
Machinery: **Geared Turbines**	*Launched:* **February 1930**
Armour (belt): **76.2mm (3in)**	*Speed:* **32.7 knots**

A heavy cruiser of the "Northampton" class, the USS *Augusta* (CA31) was launched on 1 February 1930 and was fitted out to perform the role of flagship, as were two others of her class, *Chicago* and *Houston*.

She saw her early war service in the Atlantic, and in November 1942 she was one of the warships covering the Allied Western Task Force, landing troops on the west coast of Morocco as part of Operation Torch, the Allied invasion of North Africa. This was a relatively easy landing, with the enemy having little in the way of aircraft or naval assets.

In July 1943, as part of a plan to divert the Germans' attention from the Mediterranean, where the Allies were about to land on Sicily, she accompanied the US battleships *Alabama* and *South Dakota*, then based at Scapa Flow in the Orkney Islands, as they carried out a feint operation towards the coast of Norway, together with British battleships and aircraft carriers. In June 1944, during the Allied landings in Normandy, she was the flagship of Admiral Kirk, commanding the Western Task Force, and in August she provided fire support during the landing of the 1st Special Force on the island of Levante, off the Mediterranean coast of France. She remained in service after the war, and was finally broken up in 1960.

CHICAGO

L ike *Augusta* and *Houson*, the "Northampton"-class
heavy cruiser USS *Chicago* was equipped as a flagship,
having extra accommodation for an admiral and his
battle staff. Like most US ships of the period, she had
good armament against enemy aircraft. She was
launched on 10 April 1930. On 7 December 1941 she
was escorting the aircraft carrier *Lexington,* ferrying
aircraft to Midway Island, and so escaped the Japanese
attack on Pearl Harbor.

Early in 1942 she formed part of a combined
Australian, American and New Zealand naval squadron
operating in the southwest Pacific, and was present at the
Battle of the Coral Sea in May. In June 1942, the
squadron to which Chicago belonged was designated
Task Force 44 under Rear-Admiral Crutchley, RN, and in
August it formed the Southern Covering Force during
the American landings on Guadalcanal.

On the night of 9 August 1942, *Chicago* was badly
damaged by torpedoes from Japanese warships passing
through the narrows between Savo Island and
Guadalcanal. After repair, she was assigned to Task Force
18, escorting supply convoys to Guadalcanal. On 29
January 1943 she was damaged in a heavy torpedo attack
by Japanese aircraft, and sunk in a second attack the
next day.

SPECIFICATIONS

CHICAGO

Type: **Heavy Cruiser**	Armour (deck): **76.2mm (3in)**
Length: **182.88m (600ft)**	Armour (turrets): **38.1mm (1.5in)**
Beam: **20.19m (66.25ft)**	Guns: **9x8in; 8x5in**
Draught: **7.01m (23ft)**	AA guns: **32x40mm; 27x20mm**
Displacement (normal): **9195tnes (9050t)**	Aircraft: **Four**
Displacement (full load): **12,497tnes (12,300t)**	Crew: **872**
Machinery: **Geared Turbines**	Launched: **April 1930**
Armour (belt): **76.2mm (3in)**	Speed: **32.7 knots**

DENVER

SPECIFICATIONS

DENVER

Type: **Light Cruiser**	Armour (deck): **76.2mm (3in)**
Length: **185.31m (608ft)**	Armour (turrets): **127mm (5in)**
Beam: **19.35m (63.5ft)**	Guns: **12x6in; 12x5in**
Draught: **6.7m (22ft)**	AA guns: **8x40mm; 19x20mm**
Displacement (normal): **10,160tnes (10,000t)**	Aircraft: **Three**
Displacement (full load): **14,109tnes (13,887t)**	Crew: **900**
Machinery: **Steam Turbines**	Launched: **April 1942**
Armour (belt): **127mm (5in)**	Speed: **33 knots**

One of the large "Cleveland-Fargo" class of light cruisers, the USS *Denver* (CL58) was launched on 4 April 1942. For a light vessel she was well armed, and would prove her worth during the Pacific conflict.

She went into action in the South Pacific in March 1943 as part of Task Force 68, bombarding Japanese airfields in New Georgia and participating in an action that resulted in the sinking of two Japanese destroyers. In November 1943, now assigned to Task Force 39, she was one of the warships covering the American landing in Bougainville (part of the Solomon Islands group), and in September–October 1944, with Task Force 31, she lent her fire support to the landings in the Palau group of atolls.

The provision of fire support continued to be *Denver*'s main task throughout the remainder of the Pacific war, from Leyte Gulf in October 1944 through to her final operations, the bombardment of Japanese mainland targets on Southern Honshu in July 1945.

Her bombardment actions in the interim period, covering amphibious landings while attached to various task groups, included Mindoro, Lingayen Gulf, Palawan, Mindanao and Okinawa. *Denver* survived the war despite her many major engagements, and was finally scrapped in November 1960.

DUANE

The United States Coast Guard cutter *Duane* was one of seven vessels in the "Treasury" class, so called because the ships were named after former Secretaries of the Treasury. They were large gunboats, and rendered excellent service on convoy escort duty in World War II, despite their relatively light armament and their small dimensions.

Duane was launched on 3 June 1936. One of the class, the *Alexander Hamilton*, was sunk off Reykjavik by the *U132* on 29 January 1942; the surviving boats were used as convoy flagships during up to 1944, and as amphibious force flagships in 1944–45.

Some of *Duane*'s convoy escort duties took her into the Mediterranean; for example, on 19–20 April 1944 she led a strongly-escorted convoy, UGS38, through the Straits of Gibraltar.

The 87-ship convoy was heavily attacked from the air, two freighters and the destroyer USS *Lansdale* being sunk. During the Allied landings in southern France in August 1944, *Duane* was the flagship of Rear-Admiral Lowry, commanding Task Force 84. The ships reverted to gunboat status and resumed their normal coast guard duties in 1946. Remarkably, *Duane* and four other vessels of the class remained active until the 1980s, giving good service until they were retired.

SPECIFICATIONS

DUANE

Type: **Coast Guard Cutter**	*Armour (deck):* **None**
Length: **99.66m (327ft)**	*Armour (turrets):* **N/A**
Beam: **12.49m (41ft)**	*Guns:* **2x6pdr; 1x1pdr**
Draught: **3.81m (12.5ft)**	*AA guns:* **None**
Displacement (normal): **2252tnes (2216t)**	*Aircraft:* **One**
Displacement (full load): **2388tnes (2350t)**	*Crew:* **123**
Machinery: **Geared Turbines**	*Launched:* **June 1936**
Armour (belt): **88.9mm (3.5in)**	*Speed:* **19.5 knots**

ENTERPRISE

SPECIFICATIONS

ENTERPRISE

Type: **Aircraft Carrier**	Armour (deck): **None**
Length: **246.58m (809ft)**	Armour (turrets): **N/A**
Beam: **29.1m (95.5ft)**	Guns: **8x5in; 40x40mm**
Draught: **6.52m (21.4ft)**	AA guns: **16x1.1in; 25x.5in**
Displacement (normal): **20,218tnes (19,900t)**	Aircraft: **100**
Displacement (full load): **25,892tnes (25,484t)**	Crew: **2702**
Machinery: **Geared Turbines**	Launched: **October 1936**
Armour (belt): **101.6mm (4in)**	Speed: **34 knots**

The USS *Enterprise* (CV-6) was a sister vessel of the *Yorktown* and *Hornet* and was a progressive development of the *Ranger* type. She was launched on 3 October 1936 and completed in May 1938, sailing to join the US Pacific Fleet at Pearl Harbor. She was to become one of th emost famous US aircraft carriers to see action in the Pacific.

As the flagship of Task Force 8 under Vice-Admiral Halsey, she was at sea when the Japanese attacked, delivering aircraft to Wake Island. In April 1942 she escorted the USS *Hornet* on the famous Tokyo raid, when *Hornet* flew off B-25 bombers to attack the Japanese capital. During the Battle of Midway *Enterprise*'s torpedo bombers suffered terrible casualties, but her dive bombers and those of her sister ships sank three Japanese carriers, changing the course of the war. On 24 August 1942 *Enterprise* was hit by three bombs during the Battle of the Eastern Solomons, losing 74 dead, and on 26 October she took two bomb hits at the Battle of Santa Cruz, with 44 dead.

She was present at all the US Navy's subsequent Pacific campaigns, surviving two damaging attacks by *kamikazes* off Okinawa in April and May 1945. After the war she served as an attack carrier and as an anti-submarine warfare carrier, and was broken up in 1957.

HEERMAN

The USS *Heermann* (DD532) was one of the very numerous "Fletcher" class destroyers, a highly successful design that became the backbone of the US Pacific Fleet in World War II. In all, 360 were built. *Heermann* was launched on 5 December 1942 and first went into action in November 1943 during Operation Galvanic, the American landings on Tarawa and other islands in the Gilbert group (during which the US ground forces suffered grievous losses). During this operation, she gave fire support to the US 2nd Marine Division, which experienced some of the bitterest fighting of the war on Tarawa. In October 1944 *Heermann* took part in the Battle of Leyte Gulf, and in March 1945 she was part of the large number of warships escorting carriers whose air groups made the first major raid on the Japanese Home Islands. On 17 April 1945 she assisted in the sinking of the Japanese submarine *I-56* off Okinawa.

In the closing weeks of the war, she again formed part of the escort force for aircraft carriers and battleships raiding the Japanese mainland alomst at will, and in August she was at the forefront of Task Force 38, which sailed into Sagami Bay to receive the Japanese surrender. In August 1961 *Heermann* was sold to Argentina as the *Almirante Brown*.

SPECIFICATIONS

HEERMAN

Type: **Destroyer**	*Armour (deck):* **12.7mm (.5in)**
Length: **114.75m (375.5ft)**	*Armour (turrets):* **12.7mm (.5in)**
Beam: **12.03m (39.5ft)**	*Guns:* **5x5in**
Draught: **3.81m (12.5ft)**	*AA guns:* **6x40mm; 10x20mm**
Displacement (normal): **2173tnes (2050t)**	*Aircraft:* **None**
Displacement (full load): **2540tnes (2500t)**	*Crew:* **353**
Machinery: **Steam Turbines**	*Launched:* **December 1942**
Armour (belt): **19mm (.75in)**	*Speed:* **36.5 knots**

HORNET

SPECIFICATIONS

HORNET

Type: **Aircraft Carrier**	Armour (deck): **None**
Length: **246.58m (809ft)**	Armour (turrets): **N/A**
Beam: **25.4m (83.34ft)**	Guns: **8x5in**
Draught: **6.52m (21.4ft)**	AA guns: **16x1.1in; 24x40mm**
Displacement (normal): **20,218tnes (19,900t)**	Aircraft: **100**
Displacement (full load): **25,892tnes (25,484t)**	Crew: **2702**
Machinery: **Geared Turbines**	Launched: **December 1940**
Armour (belt): **101.6mm (4in)**	Speed: **34 knots**

The third vessel of the "Yorktown" class, the USS *Hornet* (CV-7) differed from her sister ships *Yorktown* and *Enterprise* in having a larger flight deck and two catapults. Laid down at Newport News in September 1939, she was launched on 14 December 1940 and completed in October 1941.

In April 1942 she leapt to fame as the carrier that launched 16 B-25 bombers, led by Lt-Col Jimmy Doolittle, to attack Tokyo. Although the raids did little material damage, they persuaded the Japanese to make further Pacific conquests in order to extend their perimeter. This resulted in over-extended supply lines on which their merchant fleet was decimated by American submarines. *Hornet* saw action at the Battle of Midway, in which her torpedo squadrons suffered heavy casualties, but her dive bombers contributed to the sinking of three Japanese carriers.

In October 1942 she provided escort to convoys resupplying the garrison on Guadalcanal, the scene of fierce fighting. On 26 October 1942, during the Battle of Santa Cruz, *Hornet* was hit by four bombs and two torpedoes, as well as two crashing aircraft, and was again damaged by another torpedo in a second attack. She was abandoned, having lost 111 of her crew, and later sunk by Japanese destroyers.

HOUSTON

The heavy cruiser USS *Houston* (CA30) was one of the six "Northampton" class vessels. Built at Newport News, she was launched on 7 September 1929. In December 1941, as flagship of the American Task Force 5, she was engaged in escort duty in the southwest Pacific, and early in February 1942 she formed part of the Allied naval forces operating off the Dutch East Indies. On 4 February the ships were sighted by a strong force of Japanese bombers, and in the ensuing attack one of *Houston*'s 203mm (8in) gun turrets was blown off (though considering the size of air fleet, she had been lucky not to have been sunk). Despite this damage she was in action later in the month, forming part of the Allied naval force under the command of the Dutch Admiral Karel Doorman.

At the end of March, in what became known as the Battle of Sunda Strait, *Houston* and other warships attempted to intercept Japanese invasion forces landing troops on Java. *Houston* and the Australian cruiser *Perth* managed to sink two large troops transports and damage a destroyer and a minesweeper, but in a fierce gun and torpedo exchange between the Allied warships and enemy cruisers and destroyers, *Houston* and *Perth* were both sunk. The Battle of the Java Sea was a complete disaster for Allied naval power.

SPECIFICATIONS

HOUSTON

Type: **Heavy Cruiser**	Armour (deck): **76.2mm (3in)**
Length: **182.88m (600ft)**	Armour (turrets): **38.1mm (1.5in)**
Beam: **20.19m (66.25ft)**	Guns: **9x8in; 8x5in**
Draught: **7.01m (23ft)**	AA guns: **32x40mm; 27x20mm**
Displacement (normal): **9195tnes (9050t)**	Aircraft: **Four**
Displacement (full load): **12,497tnes (12,300t)**	Crew: **872**
Machinery: **Geared Turbines**	Launched: **September 1929**
Armour (belt): **76.2mm (3in)**	Speed: **32.7 knots**

INDIANAPOLIS

SPECIFICATIONS

INDIANAPOLIS

Type: **Heavy Cruiser**	Armour (deck): **101.6mm (4in)**
Length: **185.92m (610ft)**	Armour (turrets): **63.5mm (2.5in)**
Beam: **20.11m (66ft)**	Guns: **9x8in; 8x5in**
Draught: **6.7m (22ft)**	AA guns: **24x40mm; 28x20mm**
Displacement (normal): **10,008tnes (9850t)**	Aircraft: **Two**
Displacement (full load): **13,970tnes (13,750t)**	Crew: **876**
Machinery: **Geared Turbines**	Launched: **November 1931**
Armour (belt): **127mm (5in)**	Speed: **32.7 knots**

The heavy cruiser USS *Indianapolis* was one of two vessels that were improvements on the "Northampton" class, the other being the USS *Portland*. Launched on 7 November 1931, *Indianapolis* fought her way through the Pacific War from the beginning almost to the very end, when she was lost literally in the last days of hostilities.

Her battle honours included the Coral Sea, Midway, the Eastern Solomons, Santa Cruz, the Gilbert Islands, Kwajalein, Eniwetok, Palau, Leyte Gulf, Midoro Lingayen, Iwo Jima, the Marianas and Okinawa, where she was damaged by a *kamikaze* attack on 30 March 1945. In addition, she took part in numerous raids on Japanese-held islands in the Pacific, 1942–44. She seemed to live a charmed life, but her luck was about to run out.

In July 1945 she transported components of the atomic bombs from San Francisco to Tinian. On the night of 29/30 July, having delivered this vital cargo, she was proceeding to Leyte when she was hit by a salvo of six torpedoes from the Japanese submarine *I-58* and sunk with the loss of all but 316 of her 1199 crew, the survivors being picked up by American flying boats and destroyers between 2 August and 8 August. Many survived the attack, only to fall victim to sharks.

JOHNSTON

The "Fletcher"-class destroyer USS *Johnston* was launched on 25 March 1943. In January 1944 she formed part of Task Force 53 under Rear-Admiral Connolly, which landed the 4th Marine Division on Roi atoll in the Central Pacific, and in July she was part of the escort for Task Group 53.2 under Rear-Admiral Reifsnider, which landed the 1st Marine Brigade and elements of the 77th Infantry Division on Guam.

During the Battle of Leyte in October 1944 she was one of seven destroyers assigned to Rear-Admiral Sprague's Task Unit 3. On 24 October, Sprague's force intercepted a force of Japanese warships attempting to escape to Leyte Gulf through the San Bernadino Strait; torpedoes from the *Johnston* and another destroyer, the *Hoel*, hit the Japanese cruiser *Kumano* and brought her to a standstill. Shortly afterwards, however, the *Johnston* and *Hoel* came under heavy and effective fire from the Japanese battleships *Yamato* and *Nagato* and both were sunk, together with the destroyer *Samuel B. Roberts* and the escort carrier *Gambier Bay*.

The Battle of Leyte Gulf, which witnessed heavy losses on both sides, was the first occasion on which organized *kamikaze* attacks were made. Like many such attacks, their psychological value was greater than the material damage they inflicted.

SPECIFICATIONS

JOHNSTON

Type: **Destroyer**	*Armour (deck):* **12.7mm (.5in)**
Length: **114.75m (376.5ft)**	*Armour (turrets):* **12.7mm (.5in)**
Beam: **12.03m (39.5ft)**	*Guns:* **5x5in**
Draught: **3.81m (12.5ft)**	*AA guns:* **6x40mm; 10x20mm**
Displacement (normal): **2083tnes (2050t)**	*Aircraft:* **None**
Displacement (full load): **2540tnes (2500t)**	*Crew:* **358**
Machinery: **Steam Turbines**	*Launched:* **March 1943**
Armour (belt): **19mm (.75in)**	*Speed:* **36.5 knots**

LEXINGTON

SPECIFICATIONS

LEXINGTON

Type: **Aircraft Carrier**	Armour (deck): **76.2mm (3in)**
Length: **270.66m (888ft)**	Armour (turrets): **N/A**
Beam: **32.3m (106ft)**	Guns: **8x8in; 12x5in**
Draught: **7.34m (24.1ft)**	AA guns: **16x1.1in; 16x.5in**
Displacement (normal): **33,528tnes (33,000t)**	Aircraft: **80–90**
Displacement (full load): **44,094tnes (43,400t)**	Crew: **1899**
Machinery: **Express Boilers**	Launched: **October 1925**
Armour (belt): **152.4mm (6in)**	Speed: **33 knots**

America's second aircraft carrier, the USS *Lexington* was originally ordered as a battlecruiser named *Constitution*, but was renamed *Lexington* in December 1917. In July 1922 she was re-ordered as an aircraft carrier (CV-2) and launched on 3 October 1925. She appeared in US Fleet exercises for the first time in January 1929, together with her sister ship *Saratoga* (CV-3). In December 1929, she made headlines when she served as a floating power plant for the city of Tacoma, Washington, following a massive power failure. Her career during World War II was to prove that aircraft carriers, now the caital ships of the fleet, could also be vulnerable to enemy aircraft.

After the Japanese attack on Pearl Harbor her air group was involved in the battle for Wake Island, followed by convoy escort duty. In May 1942 she was operating as part of Task Force 11, a joint Allied naval force formed to prevent a Japanese landing at Port Moresby, New Guinea. In the Battle of the Coral Sea, which began in the morning of 8 May 1942 after the opposing carrier task forces sighted one another and launched their respective strike forces, *Lexington* was hit by two torpedoes and three bombs and had to be abandoned, being sunk later by the destroyer USS *Phelps*. Casualties included 216 dead.

MARYLAND

The battleship USS *Maryland* (BB46) was one of a class of four, the others being the *Colorado, Washington* and *West Virginia*. They were built in response to a new Japanese naval construction programme, although *Washington* was not completed in order to comply with the terms of the Washington Naval Treaty. *Maryland* was launched on 20 March 1920 and completed in July 1921, joining the US Pacific Fleet in the following year.

On 7 December 1941 she was damaged in the Japanese attack on Pearl Harbor (being one of the vessels neatly lined up for the Japanese aircraft that attacked the base), and while she was undergoing repair at Bremerton her anti-aircraft armament was increased, among other improvements. This turned her into a powerful vessel.

On 22 June 1944, off Saipan, she was damaged by an aircraft torpedo which hit her in the bow, and was again damaged in a *kamikaze* attack off Leyte on 29 November, 31 crew members being killed. During the subsequent repair and refit she underwent further modification, including the replacement of her secondary armament. On 7 April 1945 she was seriously damaged by a *kamikaze* off Okinawa, effectively putting her out of the war. She was decommissioned in 1947 and broken up in 1959.

SPECIFICATIONS

MARYLAND

Type: **Battleship**	*Armour (deck):* **88.9mm (3.5in)**
Length: **190.34m (624.5ft)**	*Armour (turrets):* **457.2mm (18in)**
Beam: **29.71m (97.5ft)**	*Guns:* **8x16in; 12x5in; 4x3in**
Draught: **10.69m (35.1ft)**	*AA guns:* **8x.5in**
Displacement (normal): **33,020tnes (32,500t)**	*Aircraft:* **None**
Displacement (full load): **38,100tnes (37,500t)**	*Crew:* **1500**
Machinery: **Geared Turbines**	*Launched:* **March 1920**
Armour (belt): **342.9m (13.5in)**	*Speed:* **21 knots**

MISSOURI

SPECIFICATIONS

MISSOURI

Type: **Battleship**	*Armour (deck):* **127mm (5in)**
Length: **270.35m (887ft)**	*Armour (turrets):* **431.8mm (17in)**
Beam: **32.91m (108ft)**	*Guns:* **9x16in; 20x5in**
Draught: **11.27m (37ft)**	*AA guns:* **80x40mm; 60x20mm**
Displacement (normal): **45,720tnes (45,000t)**	*Aircraft:* **Three**
Displacement (full load): **60,280tnes (59,331t)**	*Crew:* **1851**
Machinery: **Geared Turbines**	*Launched:* **January 1944**
Armour (belt): **309.88mm (12.2in)**	*Speed:* **33 knots**

The USS *Missouri* (BB-63) was one of six "Iowa"-class battleships, two of which (*Illinois* and *Kentucky*) were not completed. They were the fastest battleships ever built, with a high length to beam ratio. *Missouri* was launched on 29 January 1944 and completed in June of that year. She joined the Pacific Fleet in time to take part in the first major carrier air raids on the Japanese mainland in March 1945, forming part of the escort force. In many ways these ships were the ultimate in battleship design, but were obsolete even before they left the shipyard.

On 24 March, together with the battleships *Wisconsin* and *New Jersey*, she shelled the island of Okinawa as part of the softening-up operation prior to the American landing. During the landing phase of the operation, on 11 April 1945, she was damaged by a *kamikaze*, and she received moderate damage in another *kamikaze* attack on 16 April. In July she joined other capital ships in bombarding the Japanese mainland, and on 27 August she was part of the 3rd Fleet, sailing into Sagami Bay to accept the Japanese surrender, which was signed on board. *Missouri* carried out shore bombardment during the Korean War and also during the Gulf War, having been rearmed with cruise missiles. She is now a permanent memorial at Pearl Harbor.

PITTSBURGH

The heavy cruiser USS *Pittsburgh* (CA72), formerly named *Albany*, was launched on 22 February 1944. She was one of 24 planned vessels of the "Baltimore" class, and she went into action with the Pacific Fleet in March 1944, sailing from the anchorage at Ulithi Atoll as part of Admiral Mitscher's Task Force 58 to escort aircraft carriers making an attack on the Japanese Home Islands. During this action she and the cruiser *Santa Fe* rescued 1700 survivors from the aircraft carriers *Wasp* and *Franklin*, both heavily damaged by Japanese bombers (*Franklin* had 724 men killed and 265 injured).

In April 1945 *Pittsburgh* was attached to Task Group 58.2, supporting the landings on Okinawa. On 5 June, together with many other US warships, *Pittsburgh* was badly damaged in a typhoon, having 10.6m (35ft) of her bows torn away. However, her design meant she was able to withstand such damage. And it also gave the class long service life.

After repair *Pittsburgh* was returned to active duty and remained in service for many years after the war, being stricken in 1973. Of the original 24 vessels of the "Baltimore" class laid down, six were cancelled in August 1945 with the end of the war in the Pacific. Some, including *Pittsburgh*, were extensively modernized in the 1960s.

SPECIFICATIONS

PITTSBURGH

Type: **Heavy Cruiser**	*Armour (deck):* **65mm (2.56mm)**
Length: **205.13m (673ft)**	*Armour (turrets):* **211.32mm (8.32in)**
Beam: **21.25m (69.75ft)**	*Guns:* **9x8in; 12x5in**
Draught: **6.55m (21.5ft)**	*AA guns:* **48x40mm; 26x20mm**
Displacement (normal): **13,838tnes (13,620t)**	*Aircraft:* **Four**
Displacement (full load): **17,475tnes (17,200t)**	*Crew:* **1200**
Machinery: **Steam Turbines**	*Launched:* **February 1944**
Armour (belt): **154.43mm (6.08in)**	*Speed:* **33 knots**

RANGER

SPECIFICATIONS

RANGER

Type: **Aircraft Carrier**	Armour (deck): **25.4mm (1in)**
Length: **234.39m (769ft)**	Armour (turrets): **N/A**
Beam: **24.44m (80.2ft)**	Guns: **8x5in**
Draught: **5.94m (19.5ft)**	AA guns: **16x1.1in; 16x.5in**
Displacement (normal): **14,732tnes (14,500t)**	Aircraft: **70**
Displacement (full load): **18,288tnes (18,000t)**	Crew: **1788**
Machinery: **Geared Turbines**	Launched: **February 1933**
Armour (belt): **25.4mm (1in)**	Speed: **30.36 knots**

The only large carrier in the Atlantic Fleet, *Ranger* led the task force that provided air superiority during the amphibious invasion of French Morocco on 8 November 1942, launching 496 combat sorties in the three-day operation. Following training in Chesapeake Bay, the carrier underwent overhaul in the Norfolk Navy Yard from 16 December 1942 to 7 February 1943. She next transported 75 P-40-L army aircraft to Africa, arriving at Casablanca on 23 February; then patrolled and trained pilots along the New England coast. Departing Halifax on 11 August, she joined the British Home Fleet at Scapa Flow on 19 August.

Ranger departed Scapa Flow with the Home Fleet on 2 October to attack German shipping in Norwegian waters. Her aircraft severely damaged a German tanker, a small troop transport, four small merchantmen, a freighter and a small coaster. She did not sustain any damage during this period.

Ranger returned to Scapa Flow on 6 October 1943, and patrolled with the British Second Battle Squadron until the end of the year. In 1944 she was used for training and then underwent a major refit. Operating out of San Diego, she continued training air groups and squadrons along the peaceful California coast for the rest of the war.

SARATOGA

The USS *Saratoga* (CV-3), sister ship to the *Lexington*, was originally laid down as a battlecruiser in 1920. She was reordered as an aircraft carrier in July 1922, when she was one-third complete, and launched on 7 April 1925. Completed in 1928, she joined the Pacific Fleet in the following year. At the time of the Japanese attack on Pearl Harbor she was transporting fighters to Wake Island and consequently escaped, but on 11 January 1942 she was torpedoed by the Japanese submarine *I-6* 800km (500 miles) southwest of Oahu. Her damage was not major, though.

After repair, in June 1942, she joined Admiral Fitch's Task Force 11, but in August she was again torpedoed, this time by the *I-26*. After further repairs she subsequently operated off Guadalcanal. She provided valuable air cover for US ships operating in the area, as well as flying sorties against the enemy.

Her battle honours included the Battle of the Eastern Solomons, the Rabaul raids, the Gilbert Islands, Kwajalein and Eniwetok; she also served with the British Eastern Fleet in the Indian Ocean in 1944, her air group participating in attacks on Sabang. On 21 February 1945 she was severely damaged when hit by four *kamikazes*, putting her out of the war. On 25 July 1946, her hulk was destroyed in the atomic tests at Bikini.

SPECIFICATIONS

SARATOGA

Type: **Aircraft Carrier**	*Armour (deck):* **76.2mm (3in)**
Length: **270.66m (888ft)**	*Armour (turrets):* **N/A**
Beam: **32.3m (106ft)**	*Guns:* **8x8in; 18x5in; 12x5in**
Draught: **7.34m (24.1ft)**	*AA guns:* **16x1.1in; 30x20mm**
Displacement (normal): **33,528tnes (33,000t)**	*Aircraft:* **80–90**
Displacement (full load): **44,094tnes (43,400t)**	*Crew:* **1890**
Machinery: **Electric Turbines**	*Launched:* **April 1925**
Armour (belt): **152.4mm (6in)**	*Speed:* **33 knots**

SOUTH DAKOTA

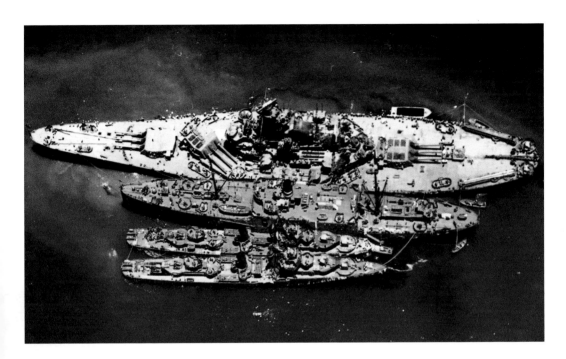

SPECIFICATIONS

SOUTH DAKOTA

Type: **Battleship**	Armour (deck): **38.1mm (1.5in)**
Length: **207.26m (680ft)**	Armour (turrets): **457.2mm (18in)**
Beam: **32.91m (108ft)**	Guns: **9x16in; 20x5in**
Draught: **11.06m (36.3ft)**	AA guns: **24x40mm; 35x20mm**
Displacement (normal): **35,116tnes (34,563t)**	Aircraft: **None**
Displacement (full load): **46,957tnes (46,218t)**	Crew: **1793**
Machinery: **Geared Turbines**	Launched: **June 1941**
Armour (belt): **309.88mm (12.2in)**	Speed: **27.8 knots**

The USS *South Dakota* (BB-57) – the largest of the four vessels in the above potograph – was leader of a class of four battleships, the others being *Alabama, Indiana* and *Massachusetts*. Built at the New York Shipyard, she was launched on 7 June 1941 and completed in March the following year. She was one of the great US battleships of the war.

In September 1942 she suffered hull damage when she struck an uncharted rock in the Tonga Islands, but was repaired in time to see action at the Battle of Santa Cruz, being damaged by a bomb hit in 'A' turret on 26 October. A week later she suffered further damage in a collision with the destroyer *Mahan*, and was again damaged by gunfire on 15 November at the Battle of Guadalcanal, suffering 38 dead.

After this somewhat unfortunate start she went on to acquire an impressive number of battle honours in the Pacific War, taking part in all the US Navy's major operations. She suffered two further mishaps, being hit by a bomb off Saipan on 19 June 1944 with the loss of 27 members of her crew, and damaged by a powder explosion in one of her gun turrets on 6 May 1945. She was present at the Japanese surrender in Sagami Bay on 2 September. *South Dakota* was decommissioned in January 1947 and broken up in 1962.

TEXAS

The USS *Texas* (BB-35) was a Dreadnought-type battleship of the "New York" class, laid down in 1911. She was launched on 18 May 1912 and completed in March 1914. During World War I she was attached to the Royal Navy's Grand Fleet for convoy protection duty in the North Atlantic, operating from Scapa Flow naval base in the Orkneys, and while she was in British waters she became the first US battleship to be fitted with a flying-off platform for spotter aircraft.

From 1919 to 1925 she served with the Pacific Fleet, rejoining the Atlantic Fleet in 1927 after undergoing a period of reconstruction. During World War II, by which time she was obsolete, she again served on convoy protection duty in the Atlantic, and provided fire support for the landings in North Africa in November 1942 and for the D-Day landings in Normandy, June 1944.

During the latter operations, she was damaged by gunfire from a shore battery at Cherbourg. After supporting the Allied landings in the south of France in August 1944 she was transferred to the Pacific, where she provided gunfire support for the American landings on the islands of Iwo Jima and Okinawa. *Texas* was stricken in April 1948 and preserved as a memorial at Galveston, Texas.

SPECIFICATIONS

TEXAS

Type: **Dreadnought**	Armour (deck): **63.5mm (2.5in)**
Length: **174.65m (573ft)**	Armour (turrets): **355.6mm (14in)**
Beam: **29.62m (97.2ft)**	Guns: **10x14in; 37x5in**
Draught: **9.6m (31.5ft)**	AA guns: **8x3in; 8x.5in**
Displacement (normal): **24,432tnes (27,000t)**	Aircraft: **None**
Displacement (full load): **28,956tnes (28,500t)**	Crew: **1054**
Machinery: **Boilers**	Launched: **May 1912**
Armour (belt): **304.8mm (12in)**	Speed: **21 knots**

TUSCALOOSA

SPECIFICATIONS

TUSCALOOSA

Type: **Heavy Cruiser**	Armour (deck): **127mm (5in)**
Length: **179.22m (588ft)**	Armour (turrets): **152.4mm (6in)**
Beam: **18.66m (61.25ft)**	Guns: **9x8in; 8x5in**
Draught: **7.01m (23ft)**	AA guns: **16x40mm; 19x20mm**
Displacement (normal): **10,109tnes (9950t)**	Aircraft: **Four**
Displacement (full load): **13,411tnes (13,200t)**	Crew: **876**
Machinery: **Geared Turbines**	Launched: **November 1933**
Armour (belt): **127mm (5in)**	Speed: **30 knots**

A "New Orleans"-class heavy cruiser, the USS *Tuscaloosa* (CA37) was launched on 15 November 1933. In the early months of World War II she took part in the US patrols in the Atlantic, ranging from Bermuda to the Denmark Strait, and from November 1941 she joined with heavy units of the Royal Navy to counter the expected breakout of the German battleship *Tirpitz* into the North Atlantic (which in the event never happened). In the summer of 1942 she escorted Arctic convoys to Russia, and in November she was one of the warships covering the Allied landings in North Africa, which were relatively easy.

In October 1943 she formed part of an Anglo-American naval force that landed Norwegian troops on the island of Spitzbergen, and later took part in raids on the Norwegian coast.

During the Normandy landings she supported the assault on "Utah" Beach, and in August covered the landings on the French Riviera. At the end of 1944 she was transferred to the Pacific Theatre, where she lent fire support to the American landings on Iwo Jima and Okinawa. *Tuscaloosa* was scrapped at Baltimore in 1959. Three of this class, *Astoria*, *Quincy* and *Vincennes*, were sunk in a cruiser battle off Guadalcanal on 9 August 1942.

YORKTOWN

The aircraft carrier USS *Yorktown* (CV-5) was launched on 4 April 1936 and completed in September of the following year. Her early service was with the Pacific Fleet, but in June 1941 she was transferred to the Atlantic for convoy protection duty. Her stay in this theatre of war was relatively short-lived, as she returned to the Pacific to form the nucleus of Task Force 17 in time to take part in raids on Japanese-held islands in the Central Pacific in January-February 1942. She was one of the greatest aircraft carriers of the war.

In March her air group was in action against Japanese forces landing in New Guinea, and in May she saw action at the Battle of the Coral Sea, being damaged by enemy bombs. She returned to Pearl Harbor, where repairs were made in only 48 hours, and on 28 May she sailed to intercept Japanese naval forces approaching Midway Island. During the ensuing battle, although her torpedo squadrons suffered heavily, her dive-bomber units contributed to the destruction of three Japanese aircraft carriers and therefore helped to tilt the war in the Pacific in the Americans' favour. However, aircraft from the carrier *Hiryu* hit *Yorktown* with two torpedoes and three bombs on 5 June 1942. Desperate attempts were made to save her, but she was sunk by the submarine *I-168* two days later.

SPECIFICATIONS

YORKTOWN

Type: **Aircraft Carrier**	*Armour (deck):* **None**
Length: **246.73m (809.5ft)**	*Armour (turrets):* **N/A**
Beam: **25.4m (83.34ft)**	*Guns:* **8x5in**
Draught: **6.52m (21.4ft)**	*AA guns:* **16x1.1in; 24x.5in**
Displacement (normal): **20,218tnes (19,900t)**	*Aircraft:* **100**
Displacement (full load): **25,892tnes (25,484t)**	*Crew:* **2702**
Machinery: **Geared Turbines**	*Launched:* **April 1936**
Armour (belt): **101.6mm (4in)**	*Speed:* **34 knots**

ARGONAUTE

SPECIFICATIONS

ARGONAUTE

Displacement surfaced: **640tnes (630t)**	*Performance surfaced:* **13.5 knots**
Displacement submerged: **811tnes (798t)**	*Performance submerged:* **7.5 knots**
Machinery: **two screws, diesel/electric motors; 1300/1000hp**	*Armament:* **six 550mm (21.7in) TT; one 75mm (3in) gun**
Length: **63.4m (208ft 11in)**	*Surface range:* **4260km (2300nm) at 7.5 knots**
Beam: **5.2m (17ft)**	*Crew:* **41**
Draught: **3.61m (11ft 9in)**	*Launch date:* **23 May 1929**

Rated as a second-class submarine, *Argonaute* and her four sister boats (*Arethuse, Atalante, La Sultane* and *La Vestale*) were authorized under the three successive construction programmes initiated in 1926 (two boats), 1927 (one boat) and 1929 (two boats). All five boats were built by Schneider, their design being based on the firm's earlier class of 600-tonne (590-ton) submarines.

Argonaute was laid down in April 1928 and completed some four years later in July 1932. Upon completing her trials she was assigned to the French submarine forces in the Mediterranean. *Argonaute* was based at Oran, and she was still there when France fell to Nazi Germany in June 1940.

Under the terms of the Franco–German Armistice she was handed over to the Vichy French Navy, and in November 1942 her crew actively resisted the Allied landings in North Africa, putting to sea with a few other French vessels in a futile attempt to attack the Anglo–American invasion fleet.

Argonaute and another submarine were sunk by the British warships *Achates* and *Westcott* off Oran on 8 November. One of *Argonaute*'s sister boats, *La Sultane*, subsequently served with the Allied naval forces in the Mediterranean.

CALYPSO

One of four 600-tonne (590-ton) Circe-class submarines laid down in 1923 by Schneider-Laubeuf, *Calypso* was completed in 1929. These second-class boats were well-armed and manoeuvrable, but they were cramped internally and crew conditions were poor, hence the requirement for the larger 630-tonne (620-ton) class that followed them.

In addition to the four Circe class submarines, four 600-tonne (590-ton) boats (the Sirene class) were built by A.C. de la Loire and four (the Ariane class) by A.C. Augustin-Normand. Of *Calypso*'s sister boats (some of which are shown above), the *Doris* became an early war casualty. In April 1940, while serving with the 10th Submarine Flotilla, she deployed to Harwich together with five other French submarines to reinforce the Royal Navy's boats, and on 10 May she was sunk by the German submarine *U-9* off the Dutch coast.

The other boats of the Circe class were deployed to the Mediterranean. *Thetis* was scuttled at Toulon on 27 November 1942 just before German forces occupied the port, while *Circe* and *Calypso* were seized by the enemy at Bizerta, Tunisia, on 8 December. *Circe* was allocated to the Italian Navy and was scuttled in May 1943, while *Calypso* was destroyed in an air attack on 30 January of that year.

SPECIFICATIONS

CALYPSO

Displacement surfaced: **625tnes (615t)**	Performance surfaced: **14 knots**
Displacement submerged: **788tnes (776t)**	Performance submerged: **7.5 knots**
Machinery: **two screws, diesel- electric motors, 1250/1000hpp**	Armament: **seven 550mm (21.7in) TT; one 75mm (3in) gun**
Length: **62.48m (205ft)**	Surface range: **6482km (3500nm) at 10 knots**
Beam: **5.40m (17ft 9in)**	Crew: **41**
Draught: **3.90m (12ft 9in)**	Launch date: **15 January 1926**

CASABIANCA

SPECIFICATIONS

CASABIANCA

Displacement surfaced:
1595tnes (1570t)

Performance surfaced:
17–20 knots

Displacement submerged:
2117tnes (2084t)

Performance submerged:
10 knots

Machinery:
**twin screws,
diesel/electric motors;
2900/1800hp**

Armament:
**nine 550mm (21.7in)
and two 400mm
(15.7in) TT; one
100mm (3.9in) gun**

Length:
92.3m (210ft)

Surface range:
**18,530km (10,000nm)
at 10 knots**

Beam:
8.2m (18ft 7in)

Crew:
61

Draught:
4.7m (10ft 9in)

Launch date:
2 February 1935

Laid down in 1931, *Casabianca* was an ocean-going submarine of the Redoutable class. These first-class submarines, of which there were 29 in total, were double-hulled boats with excellent handling qualities and a good turn of speed on the surface.

The major drawback of Redoutable-class submarines was that it took them up to 50 seconds to dive, which was thought to be rather slow at a time when anti-submarine aircraft were presenting an increasing threat at sea.

The Redoutable-class was not without its misfortunes, either. One of the first series boats, *Promethee*, sank during a trials exercise on 8 July 1942, and another, *Phenix*, disappeared without trace off French Indo-China on 15 June 1939. Seven boats were scuttled at Toulon in November 1942 when German forces occupied the south of France, four were scuttled at Brest, and others were lost in Allied air attacks on French colonial territory. One boat, *Protee*, was probably lost in a German depth-charge attack, while *Sfax* was torpedoed in error by the German submarine *U-37* after France had surrendered.

Casabianca, along with the Free French Forces, played a major part in the liberation of Corsica, sinking a German patrol craft and damaging another.

ESPADON

The Requin ("Shark") class of nine ocean-going submarines, to which *Espadon* ("Swordfish") belonged, were the first of their type to be designed in France after World War I, and their technology incorporated a great deal gleaned from the study of captured German U-boats in that conflict.

The Requin class carried a heavy offensive armament, with four bow, two stern and two twin torpedo tubes mounted in containers in the casing. These could be remotely trained either submerged or on the surface, but could not be reloaded at sea. The boats were double-hulled and had a diving depth of 80m (250ft). All the Requin class boats were fully refitted and modernized between 1935 and 1937.

Eight of the group were lost during World War II. On 8 December 1942, *Espadon* was one of four boats captured by the Italians at Bizerta; she was subsequently commissioned by the Italian Navy as the *FR114*, and on 13 September 1943 she was scuttled by the Germans at Castellammare di Stabia while being converted as a transport submarine.

The same fate was to befall two of *Espadon*'s sisters, *Requin* and *Dauphin*. Another boat, *Phoque*, became operational with the Italian Navy and was sunk in an air attack.

SPECIFICATIONS

ESPADON

Displacement surfaced:
1168tnes (1150t)

Displacement submerged:
1464tnes (1441t)

Machinery:
twin screws,
diesel/electric motors;
2900/1800hp

Length:
78.2m
(256ft 9in)

Beam:
6.8m (22ft 5in)

Draught:
5m (16ft 9in)

Performance surfaced:
15 knots

Performance submerged:
9 knots

Armament:
10 533mm
(21in) TT; one
100mm (3.9in) gun

Surface range:
10,469km (5650nm)
at 10 knots

Crew:
54

Launch date:
28 May 1926

JUNON

SPECIFICATIONS

JUNON

Displacement surfaced: **672tnes (662t)**	*Performance surfaced:* **15 knots**
Displacement submerged: **869tnes (856t)**	*Performance submerged:* **9.3 knots**
Machinery: **two screws, diesel/electric motors; 1800/1230hp**	*Armament:* **six 550mm (21.7in) and three 400mm (15.7in) TT; one 75mm (3in) gun**
Length: **68.10m (223ft 5in)**	*Surface range:* **7400km (4000nm) at 10 knots**
Beam: **5.62m (18ft 5in)**	*Crew:* **42**
Draught: **4.03m (13ft 3in)**	*Launch date:* **15 September 1935**

Authorized in 1930, the Minerve class of six submarines, *Junon* being one of them, represented a determined attempt by the French Admiralty to standardize the design of the earlier 630-tonne (620-ton) types, which had many variations despite being produced to the same specification.

Before the French collapse in 1940, *Junon* and *Minerve* managed to escape across the English Channel to Plymouth. *Minerve* had in fact been fully stripped down by the French at Cherbourg when the Germans broke through at Sedan on 19 May 1940; it was only after an epic effort by French engineers that she was made ready for sea just before the enemy arrived at the port.

Both boats subsequently served with distinction with the Free French Naval Forces, carrying out numerous war patrols in the Norwegian Sea and the Arctic. *Junon's* commander was Lt Querville.

The boat survived the war and was sold for scrap in 1954; *Minerve* was wrecked in September 1945. The other three Minerve-class boats, *Venus*, *Ceres* and *Pallas* were all scuttled in 1942, the last two at Oran, where they were later refloated and scrapped; and *Iris* sailed for Barcelona, where she was interned until the end of the war. She was broken up in 1954.

MINERVE

After her escape from Cherbourg and arrival at Plymouth (see entry for *Junon* on the previous page), *Minerve*, under the command of Lt Sonneville, joined the Scottish-based 9th Submarine Flotilla, which also included the RN submarine *Sealion* and the Dutch boats *O21* and *O23*.

Minerve's operations off the Norwegian coast began in February 1941, and on 19 April that same year, while engaged in attacking an enemy convoy, she was heavily depth-charged by German escorts and narrowly escaped being sunk.

In May 1941 *Minerve* took part in the hunt for the German battleship *Bismarck* and the heavy cruiser *Prinz Eugen*, which were attempting to break out into the North Atlantic. Together with the RN submarine *Uproar* (*P31*) she was sent north to search for the *Bismarck* after the latter had refuelled in a fjord near Bergen, but neither submarine was able to locate the elusive battleship.

Later in 1941, *Minerve* operated in concert with another French submarine, *Rubis*, and in July 1942 she operated in the Arctic with eight British submarines, stationed in two lines south of Bear Island to protect the ill-fated convoy PQ.17, which was later virtually destroyed by air and U-boat attacks.

SPECIFICATIONS

MINERVE

Displacement surfaced: **672tnes (662t)**	Performance surfaced: **15 knots**
Displacement submerged: **869tnes (856t)**	Performance submerged: **9.3 knots**
Machinery: **two screws,** **diesel/electric motors;** **1800/1230hp**	Armament: **six 550mm (21.7in) and** **three 400mm (15.7in)** **TT; one 75mm (3in) gun**
Length: **68.10m** **(223ft 5in)**	Surface range: **7400km (4000nm)** **at 10 knots**
Beam: **5.62m (18ft 5in)**	Crew: **42**
Draught: **4.03m (13ft 3in)**	Launch date: **23 October 1934**

NARVAL

SPECIFICATIONS

NARVAL

Displacement surfaced: **974tnes (990t)**	Performance surfaced: **15 knots**
Displacement submerged: **1464tnes (1441t)**	Performance submerged: **9 knots**
Machinery: **twin screws, diesel/electric motors; 2900/1800hp**	Armament: **10 550mm (21.7in) TT; one 10mm (3.9in) gun**
Length: **78.25m (256ft 7in)**	Surface range: **4262km (2300nm) at 7.5 knots**
Beam: **6.84m (22ft 6in)**	Crew: **54**
Draught: **5.10m (16ft 9in)**	Launch date: **9 May 1925**

One of the nine Requin- ("Shark"-) class submarines, *Narval* was a large boat that was intended for colonial service, long-range operations against commerce and scouting operations for the fleet. She was on station in the Mediterranean at the outbreak of World War II.

From 10 June 1940, the day Italy entered the war, she made several sorties from Tunisian ports in search of Italian shipping, but failed to make contact. On 1 July, while on war patrol, her captain was ordered by the French Naval Staff to make for the port of Toulon, where French warships were assembling in the newly created Free (Vichy) Zone under the terms of the Franco-German Armistice. He refused, and instead sailed for Malta, where *Narval* was incorporated into the Free French Naval Forces.

On 15 December 1940, *Narval* was sunk by a mine off Tunisia. It is sometimes erroneously recorded that she was sunk off Tobruk by the Italian torpedo boat *Clio* on 7 January 1941.

In January 1944, the name *Narval* was allocated to the former Italian second-class submarine *Bronzo* (shown above), which had been captured by the Royal Navy in July 1943 and later handed over to the Free French. She was used as an asdic training vessel.

ORPHEE

The Diane-class submarine *Orphee* was one of nine in that class, all completed between September 1932 and December 1934. In April 1940, together with other boats of the 10th French Submarine Flotilla and their depot ship *Jules Verne*, *Orphee* deployed to Harwich to reinforce the submarines of the British Home Fleet, beginning operations off the Dutch coast in May of that year.

Early in June 1940, following Italy's entry into the war, *Orphee* deployed to Casablanca, and so managed to escape seizure by the British. During the Allied landings in North Africa in November 1942, when four boats of the Diane class were sunk and *Diane* herself was scuttled, *Orphee* was at sea, and subsequently returned to Casablanca when the fighting was at an end.

Taken over by the Free French Navy, *Orphee* was rearmed and turned over to special duties work, carrying out many clandestine operations, including the landing and extraction of agents in the Mediterranean area. On 7 December 1943 she sank the patrol boat *Faucon* at the entrance to Toulon harbour.

Orphee survived the war and was broken up in 1946. Her two remaining sister vessels, *Antiope* and *Amazone*, were scrapped immediately after the war.

SPECIFICATIONS

ORPHEE

Displacement surfaced: 580tnes (571t)	**Performance surfaced:** 13.7 knots
Displacement submerged: 822tnes (809t)	**Performance submerged:** 9.2 knots
Machinery: twin screws, diesel/electric motors; 1300/1800hp	**Armament:** six 550mm (21.7in) TT; one 75mm (3in) gun
Length: 64.4m (211ft 4in)	**Surface range:** 7400km (4000nm) at 10 knots
Beam: 6.2m (20ft 4in)	**Crew:** 41
Draught: 4.3m (14ft 1in)	**Launch date:** 10 November 1931

PONCELET

SPECIFICATIONS

PONCELET

Displacement surfaced: **1595tnes (1570t)**	*Performance surfaced:* **17–20 knots**
Displacement submerged: **2117tnes (2084t)**	*Performance submerged:* **10 knots**
Machinery: **twin screws, diesel/electric motors; 2900/1800hp**	*Armament:* **nine 550mm (21.7in) and two 400mm (15.7in) TT; one 100mm (3.9in) gun**
Length: **92.3m (210ft)**	*Surface range:* **18,530km (10,000nm) at 10 knots**
Beam: **8.2m (18ft 7in)**	*Crew:* **61**
Draught: **4.7m (10ft 9in)**	*Launch date:* **2 February 1935**

At the beginning of World War II, together with the other Redoutable-class submarines *Agosta, Ouessant* and *Persee, Poncelet* (Cdr de Saussine) was deployed to the Azores for missions against German blockade runners operating in the area.

Poncelet had an early success when, on 28 September 1939, she captured the 5994-tonne (5900-ton) cargo ship *Chemnitz*. In August and September 1940 *Poncelet* acted in support of land operations by the Vichy French government in Libreville, Gabon, where Free French elements were attempting to take over the colonial administration.

The attempted coup failed, but in November Libreville was assaulted by troops of the French Foreign Legion under General Leclerc, supported by Free French and Royal Navy warships. In the course of this action *Poncelet* made a sortie against the Allied ships and was severely damaged by depth-charges from the British sloop HMS *Milford Haven* and, as a result, was forced to surface. Her crew scuttled her and abandoned ship, although Cdr de Saussine chose to remain on board and went down with his submarine.

Poncelet was named after General Jean-Victor Poncelet (1788–1867), the author of many works on applied mechanics.

REQUIN

The Requin ("Shark") class of nine ocean-going boats formed an important element in France's submarine strength at the outbreak of World War II, although the French boats were not all up to 1939 naval warfare standards. *Requin*'s sister submarine *Narval*, for example, reputedly had the noisiest machinery of any boat.

The strength of France's submarine force lay in its sheer size; in September 1939 France had 77 boats in commission, of which 38 were ocean-going, 32 coastal, 6 minelaying and 1 (*Surcouf*) a cruiser. Successive French governments, between the two world wars, regarded submarines as the cheapest way of exercising sea power; the dubious theory was that any nation that had a sufficient number was bound to have a degree of international influence, so planning got off to a rapid start with the Requin class, France's first post-World War I ocean-going submarines.

Requin and most of the others formed part of the Vichy French Navy after the fall of France. On 8 December 1942 she was captured at Bizerta by a small German battle group. Handed over to the Italians and designated *FR113*, she was being converted as a supply submarine when she was again seized by the Germans after Italy's surrender. She was scuttled, then later raised and scrapped.

SPECIFICATIONS

REQUIN

Displacement surfaced: 1168tnes (1150t)	**Performance surfaced:** 15 knots
Displacement submerged: 1464tnes (1441t)	**Performance submerged:** 9 knots
Machinery: twin screws, diesel/electric motors; 2900/1800hp	**Armament:** 10 533mm (21in) TT; one 100mm (3.9in) gun
Length: 78.2m (56ft 9in)	**Surface range:** 10,469km (5650nm) at 10 knots
Beam: 6.8m (22ft 5in)	**Crew:** 54
Draught: 5m (16ft 9in)	**Launch date:** 19 July 1926

RUBIS

SPECIFICATIONS

RUBIS

Displacement surfaced: **640tnes (630t)**	Performance surfaced: **13.5 knots**
Displacement submerged: **640tnes (630t)**	Performance submerged: **7.5 knots**
Machinery: **two screws, diesel/electric motors; 1300/1000hp**	Armament: **10 533mm (21in) TT; one 100mm (3.9in) gun**
Length: **63.4m (208ft 11in)**	Surface range: **4262km (2300nm) at 7.5 knots**
Beam: **5.2m (17ft)**	Crew: **41**
Draught: **3.61m (11ft 9in)**	Launch date: **23 May 1929**

Without doubt the most active and successful minelaying submarine of World War II, *Rubis* (Ruby) was one of six vessels of the Saphir class. Two of the boats were authorized in 1925, and one in each year from 1926 to 1929. They were not outstanding boats, and the key to their success was the safe and effective system of vertical external minelaying tubes, which has been developed by Normand-Fenaux. These were incorporated in the outer ballast tanks and equipped with a direct release mechanism.

In April 1940, following the German invasion of Norway, *Rubis* was one of the French submarine flotilla deployed to Harwich to work alongside Royal Navy boats. *Rubis* joined 11 French submarines of the 10th Flotilla and the 2nd Submarine Division in reinforcing British submarines at Harwich, and she began minelaying operations off Norway on 10 May, operating mainly from the Scottish port of Dundee. In July 1940, after the fall of France, *Rubis*' commanding officer and crew elected to serve with the Free French Naval Forces.

In the course of 22 sorties to Norwegian waters and the Bay of Biscay, *Rubis*' mine barrages sank 14 merchant vessels and eight small warships; she also torpedoed and sank the Finnish merchant ship *Hogland*. She was stricken in 1949.

SURCOUF

An experimental submarine, of a type that was unlikely to be repeated, *Surcouf* was designed for long-range commerce raiding, being described as a "Corsair submarine" by the French Admiralty.

The heaviest submarine in the world at the outbreak of World War II, she carried the largest calibre of guns permitted to be mounted on submarines under the terms of the Washington Treaty; they were identical to those mounted on heavy cruisers, and were mounted in a watertight turret. They had a maximum theoretical range of range of 27,450m (30,000yd) at a 30-degree elevation, although this was reduced to 12,000m (13,000yd) in practice by the limitations of the rangefinder. The guns could be ready to fire two minutes after surfacing.

In July 1940, having sought refuge in Plymouth, *Surcouf* was seized by the British. She later served with the Free French Naval Forces, carrying out patrols in the Atlantic and taking part in the capture of the islands of St Pierre and Miquelon off Newfoundland, which were opposed to General de Gaulle's French government in exile.

Surcouf was lost on 18 February 1942, in an ignominious collision with the US merchant ship *Thomson Lykes* in the Gulf of Mexico.

SPECIFICATIONS

SURCOUF

Displacement surfaced: **3302tnes (3250t)**	Performance surfaced: **18 knots**
Displacement submerged: **4373tnes (4304t)**	Performance submerged: **8.5 knots**
Machinery: **twin screws, diesel/electric motors; 7600/3400hp**	Armament: **eight 551mm (21.7in) and four 400mm (15.75in) TT; two 203mm (8in) guns,**
Length: **110m (360ft 10in)**	Surface range: **18,530km (10,000nm)**
Beam: **9.1m (29ft 9in)**	Crew: **118**
Draught: **9.07m (29ft 9in)**	Launch date: **18 October 1929**

U-30

SPECIFICATIONS

U-30

Displacement surfaced: **640tnes (630t)**	Performance surfaced: **16 knots**
Displacement submerged: **757tnes (745t)**	Performance submerged: **8 knots**
Machinery: **two screws, diesel/electric motors; 2100/750hp**	Armament: **five 533mm (21in) TT; one 88mm (3.5in) gun; one 20mm AA**
Length: **64.5m (211ft 6in)**	Surface range: **6916km (3732nm) at 12 knots**
Beam: **5.8m (19ft 3in)**	Crew: **44**
Draught: **4.4m (14ft 6in)**	Launch date: **1937**

The Type VIIA U-boat *U-30* was among the first wave of German submarines to be deployed to their operational areas in the North Atlantic just prior to the outbreak of World War II. Commanded by Lt Lemp, *U-30* was to become notorious for sinking the passenger liner *Athenia*, which Lemp mistook for an armed merchant cruiser, on 3 September 1939. Lemp sank two more merchant ships on his first war patrol, and on 28 December he torpedoed and damaged the battleship HMS *Barham*.

During the German invasion of Norway in April 1940 the *U-30* supported the German landing at Trondheim, and in July 1940 she became the first German submarine to deploy to the newly captured French base of Lorient.

In the course of several war voyages Lemp destroyed a respectable tonnage of Allied shipping before *U-30* was relegated to training duties. She was scuttled at Flensburg, northern Germany, on 5 May 1945.

After leaving *U-30* Lemp went on to command the *U-110*, losing his life when this submarine was captured by British warships, yielding at the same time a top -secret "Enigma" code machine. These German naval codes, deciphered by Allied specialists, played a major part in defeating the U-boat packs.

U-32

The Type VIIA *U-32* began her war career as part of the U-boats' East Command, operating in the Baltic in support of operations in Poland. Transferred to the North Atlantic theatre towards the end of 1939, and commanded by Lt Jenisch, *U-32* was employed on minelaying duties off the Scottish coast, Portsmouth, Liverpool and Newport. Her mine barrages are known to have claimed at least two merchant ships, and she sank two merchant vessels more in torpedo attacks in March 1940.

Operating from Lorient, *U-32* sank a further five ships on one patrol in July 1940 and six more in August. On 1 September, Jenisch carried out a successful torpedo attack on the cruiser *Fiji* west of the Hebrides, damaging the warship and forcing her to make for port. A further eight merchant ships fell victim to *U-32*'s torpedoes and gunfire in September and October 1940.

On 28 October, *U-32* attacked the passenger ship *Empress of Britain*, which had already been damaged by air attack and under tow, and sank her with two torpedoes north-west of Donegal Bay, Ireland. Two days later, in an attack on a convoy *U-32* was depth-charged and sunk by the British destroyers *Harvester* and *Highlander*.

SPECIFICATIONS

U-32

Displacement surfaced: **636tnes (626t)**	Performance surfaced: **16 knots**
Displacement submerged: **757tnes (745t)**	Performance submerged: **8 knots**
Machinery: **two screws, diesel/electric motors; 2100/750hp**	Armament: **five 533mm (21in) TT; one 88mm (3.5in) gun; one 20mm AA**
Length: **64.5m (211ft 6in)**	Surface range: **6916km (3732nm) at 12 knots**
Beam: **5.8m (19ft 3in)**	Crew: **44**
Draught: **4.4m (14ft 6in)**	Launch date: **1937**

U-39

SPECIFICATIONS

U-39

Displacement surfaced: **640tnes (630t)**	Performance surfaced: **16 knots**
Displacement submerged: **757tnes (745t)**	Performance submerged: **8 knots**
Machinery: **two screws, diesel/electric motors; 2100/750hp**	Armament: **five 533mm (21in) TT; one 88mm (3.5in) gun; one 20mm AA**
Length: **64.5m (211ft 6in)**	Surface range: **6916km (3732nm) at 12 knots**
Beam: **5.8m (19ft 3in)**	Crew: **44**
Draught: **4.4m (14ft 6in)**	Launch date: **1937**

The Type VII U-boat *U-39*, under the command of Lt-Cdr Glattes, came close to achieving a spectacular success in the first month of World War II.

U-boats operating from the north German ports were heavily engaged in minelaying operations during the early weeks of the war. These operations were taking a growing toll of Allied shipping, and to counter them the Royal Navy formed two hunting groups, each comprising an aircraft carrier and four destroyers.

On 14 September 1939, *U-39* sighted the British aircraft carrier *Ark Royal* and her hunting group to the west of the Hebrides and Glattes fired a salvo of three torpedoes at her. Fortunately for the carrier, the torpedoes were of a new type fitted with magnetic pistols. These were faulty and the torpedoes detonated prematurely.

Ark Royal's escorting destroyers, *Faulknor*, *Foxhound* and *Firedrake*, closed in and forced the U-boat to the surface with depth-charges. Her crew escaped just before she sank and were taken prisoner.

Just three days later, *U-39*'s sister boat, *U-29*, sank the aircraft carrier *Courageous*, with the loss of 514 lives. After that, the Royal Navy withdrew carriers from its anti-U-boat operations.

U-47

The *U-47* was one of 24 Type VIIB U-boats, the Type VIIB being a slightly larger version of the Type VIIA, with a greater range and slightly higher surface speed.

Commanded by Lt-Cdr Gunther Prien, the *U-47* achieved early fame in World War II when, on the night of 13/14 October 1939, having already sunk three British merchant ships, she penetrated the defences of Scapa Flow and made a daring attack on the 29,616-tonne (29,150-ton) Royal Sovereign-class battleship *Royal Oak*, a veteran of World War I, and sank her with three torpedo hits.

The attack cost the lives of more than 800 British seamen and came as a considerable blow to British morale. Prien and his crew, understandably feted as heroes by the German people, operated in support of the German invasion of Norway in April 1940 and subsequently deployed to the French Atlantic ports, where they continued to operate against British Atlantic convoys.

This excellent U-boat commander and his highly trained crew sank a further 27 ships before being lost when *U-47* was surprised in a heavy squall and depth-charged by the Royal Navy corvettes *Arbutus* and *Camellia* on the night of 7/8 March 1941.

SPECIFICATIONS

U-47

Displacement surfaced: **765tnes (753t)**	*Performance surfaced:* **17.25 knots**
Displacement submerged: **871tnes (857t)**	*Performance submerged:* **8 knots**
Machinery: **two shafts, diesel/electric motors; 2800/750hp**	*Armament:* **10 533mm (21in) TT; one 100mm (3.9in) gun**
Length: **66.5m (218ft)**	*Surface range:* **4262km (2300nm) at 7.5 knots**
Beam: **6.2m (20ft 3in)**	*Crew:* **44**
Draught: **4.7m (15ft 6in)**	*Launch date:* **1938**

U-81

SPECIFICATIONS

U-81

Displacement surfaced: **793tnes (781t)**	Performance surfaced: **17 knots**
Displacement submerged: **879tnes (871t)**	Performance submerged: **7.5 knots**
Machinery: **two shafts, diesel/electric motors; 2800/750hp**	Armament: **five 533mm (21in) TT; one 37mm (3.5in) gun; one 20mm AA**
Length: **66.5m (218ft)**	Surface range: **10,454km (5642nm) at 12 knots**
Beam: **6.2m (20ft 3in)**	Crew: **44**
Draught: **4.7m (15ft 6in)**	Launch date: **1939**

The British aircraft carrier *Ark Royal* eventually succumbed to German torpedoes, but not until November 1941, and the submarine that launched them was the *U-81*.

Under the command of Lt-Cdr Guggenberger, this Type VIIC boat began operations in the Arctic in July 1941 and narrowly escaped being sunk by a Soviet patrol vessel on her first sortie. She continued to operate in the Arctic as part of the 'Markgraf' U-boat group before deploying to the Mediterranean in October of that year.

On 13 November 1941, *Ark Royal* was returning to Gibraltar after flying off reinforcement fighters for Malta when she was attacked by *U-81*, being hit by one torpedo from a salvo of four. Despite desperate attempts to tow her to safety, she sank the following day, fortunately with the loss of only one life.

U-81 continued to operate in the Mediterranean, but did not enjoy any further success until November 1942, when she sank a transport vessel during the Allied landings in North Africa. The boat now had a new commander, Lt Krieg, but failed to achieve any major successes, her principal victims being sailing vessels, which were sunk by gunfire.

On 9 January 1944, *U-81* was destroyed in an air attack on Pola, her main operating base.

U-106

Designed for long-range operations in distant waters, the Type IXB U-boats, of which *U-106* was one, were a development of the Type IXAs but with an increased radius. Some Type IXBs were provided with extra fuel tankage, giving them enough range (16,100km [8700nm] at 12 knots) to deploy as far as Japan (presumably to attack British vessels).

Operating from bases such as Penang and Singapore, these Type IXB boats were a constant threat to Allied convoys in the Indian Ocean. The *U-106*, however, spent her entire war in the Atlantic, beginning operations early in 1941. From time to time she acted as a weather boat, her range enabling her to operate far out in the ocean.

During this period (February to April 1941) the *U-106* enjoyed considerable success under her able captain, Lt-Cdr Oesten; on the night of 19/20 March she torpedoed the battleship *Malaya*, which was escorting a convoy in the central Atlantic, causing sufficient damage to remove her from first-line service for the rest of the war.

The *U-106* continued on operations under a new captain, Lt-Cdr Rasch, and achieved further sinkings before she herself was sunk by air attack off Cape Ortegal, Biscay, on 2 August 1943.

SPECIFICATIONS

U-106

Displacement surfaced: **1068tnes (1051t)**	Performance surfaced: **18.25 knots**
Displacement submerged: **2183tnes (1178t)**	Performance submerged: **7.25 knots**
Machinery: **two shafts, diesel/electric motors; 4400/1000hp**	Armament: **six 533mm (21in) TT; one 102mm (4.1in)**
Length: **76.5m (251ft)**	Surface range: **13,993km (7552nm)**
Beam: **6.8m (22ft 3in)**	Crew: **48**
Draught: **4.6m (15ft)**	Launch date: **1939**

U-110

SPECIFICATIONS

U-110

Displacement surfaced: 1068tnes (1051t)	**Performance surfaced:** 18.25 knots
Displacement submerged: 2183tnes (1178t)	**Performance submerged:** 7.25 knots
Machinery: two shafts, diesel/electric motors; 4400/1000hp	**Armament:** six 533mm (21in) TT; one 102mm (4.1in) gun; one 20mm AA
Length: 76.5m (251ft)	**Surface range:** 13,993km (7552nm)
Beam: 6.8m (22ft 3in)	**Crew:** 48
Draught: 4.6m (15ft)	**Launch date:** 1939

On the evening of 15 March 1941, the Type IXB submarine *U-110* under the command of Lt-Cdr Julius Lemp (formerly of the *U-30*) closed in to attack a British convoy in the North Atlantic, together with several other U-boats. These included two commanded by German U-boat "aces": the *U-99* (Lt-Cdr Kretschmer) and the *U-100* (Lt-Cdr Schepke). In what turned out to be a particularly disastrous encounter with Royal Navy escort forces, *U-99* and *U-100* were both sunk, while *U-110* and the others were beaten off.

For the German submariners, it was a taste of things to come, and an indication of what a properly organized escort group could achieve.

Lemp and his crew finally met their fate on 9 May of that year, when the *U-110* closed in to make an attack on convoy HX123, south of Iceland. Lemp succeeded in sinking two ships, but depth-charges from the corvette *Aubretia* blew the *U-110* to the surface and she was abandoned by her crew, being captured intact by a boarding party from the destroyer *Bulldog*.

The British sailors seized an "Enigma" code machine and other material that was to prove priceless to British intelligence, shortly before the *U-110* sank under tow. Lt-Cdr Lemp lost his life in this incident.

U-112

The design of the Type XI U-boat *U-112* had its origins in World War I, when the German Navy enjoyed considerable success with its so-called "submarine cruisers". These were large, heavily armed boats whose tactics were to surface and sink merchant vessels with gunfire (as shown above), reserving their torpedoes for armoured warships that were able to defend themselves.

The result was that German submarines carried progressively heavier armament as their design evolved during the war years, until eventually, boats of new construction carried two 150mm (5.9in) guns and older boats were modified to bring them up to a similar standard. Guns of this calibre had a greater range than any that were mounted in merchant vessels, so the U-boat commander could stand off and sink his victim at leisure.

The concept of the submarine cruiser, which was intended for surface attacks against merchant shipping, was resurrected in World War II with the design of the German Type XI. As with the French *Surcouf*, of similar concept, provision was made for a spotter aircraft. Three boats were planned, beginning with *U-112*, but they never progressed beyond the project stage, and it was left to the Japanese to develop comparable vessels.

SPECIFICATIONS

U-112

Displacement surfaced: 3190tnes (3140t)	**Performance surfaced:** 23 knots
Displacement submerged: 3688tnes (3630t)	**Performance submerged:** 7 knots
Machinery: two shafts, diesel/electric motors	**Armament:** eight 533mm (21in) TT; four 127mm (5in) guns; two 30mm and two 20mm AA
Length: 115m (377ft)	**Surface range:** 25,266km (13,635nm) at 12 knots
Beam: 9.5m (31ft)	**Crew:** 110
Draught: 6m (20ft)	**Launch date:** Projected only

U-570

SPECIFICATIONS

U-570

Displacement surfaced: 793tnes (781t)	**Performance surfaced:** 17 knots
Displacement submerged: 879tnes (871t)	**Performance submerged:** 7.5 knots
Machinery: two shafts, diesel/electric motors; 2800/750hp	**Armament:** five 533mm (21in) TT; one 37mm (3.5in) gun; one 20mm AA
Length: 66.5m (218ft)	**Surface range:** 10,454km (5642nm) at 12 knots
Beam: 6.2m (20ft 3in)	**Crew:** 44
Draught: 4.7m (15ft 6in)	**Launch date:** 1939

On 27 August 1941 the Type VIIC submarine *U-570*, commanded by Lt Hans Rahmlow, was one of a group of U-boats operating southwest of Iceland against convoy HX145, which had been located by the German Signals Intelligence Service.

The submarine was attacked in bad weather by a Lockheed Hudson of No 269 Squadron RAF, flown by Sqn Ldr J.H. Thompson, and damaged; Rahmlow, unable to submerge, raised the flag of surrender and continued to circle the boat until relieved by a Catalina of No 209 Squadron. The armed trawler *Northern Chief* reached the scene that evening, followed by three more trawlers and the destroyers *Burwell* and *Niagara* the following day.

The submarine's crew was taken off and the *U-570* was towed to Iceland, where she was beached. Although her crew had destroyed most of the secret material on board, the capture of an intact U-boat was an important achievement.

Commissioned into the Royal Navy as HMS *Graph*, she was used for depth-charge trials, yielding information on the effects of explosions on her pressure hull. She was wrecked while on passage from Chatham to the Clyde in March 1944 and was scrapped in 1947.

U-791

In the early 1930s, the German engineer Helmuth Walter began work on a circuit motor that would function independently of oxygen derived from the atmosphere. The turbine he developed used concentrated hydrogen peroxide, which was heated via a catalyst to produce the required oxygen and high-pressure steam.

The first experimental submarine fitted with this revolutionary system, V80, was launched in January 1940 and reached the then incredible submerged speed of 28 knots.

Other experimental boats followed, culminating in the Type V300 experimental submarine *U-791*, built in 1943. However, work proceeded very slowly, not least because of problems in handling the highly unstable hydrogen peroxide and in designing an effective streamlined hull in order to achieve the desired underwater speeds. As a consequence the entire project was given low priority.

By 1943, when conventional U-boats were being defeated by Allied countermeasures in the Atlantic and Mediterranean, work was at last accelerated, but by then it was too late; it was calculated that the development of an operational long-range Walter-propelled submarine would have taken at least two years.

SPECIFICATIONS

U-791

Displacement surfaced: **609tnes (600t)**	*Performance surfaced:* **9.3 knots**
Displacement submerged: **655tnes (645t)**	*Performance submerged:* **19 knots**
Machinery: **single screw, two diesels and two Walter turbines and two electric motors; 150/2180/75hp**	*Armament:* **two 533mm (21in) TT**
Length: **52.10m (170ft 11in)**	*Surface range:* **not known**
Beam: **4.00m (13ft 1in)**	*Crew:* **25**
Draught: **5.50m (70ft)**	*Launch date:* **1943**

U-1405

SPECIFICATIONS

U-1405

Displacement surfaced: **319tnes (314t)**	*Performance surfaced:* **8.5 knots (estimated)**
Displacement submerged: **363tnes (357t)**	*Performance submerged:* **23 knots**
Machinery: **single screw, two diesels and two Walter turbines and two electric motors; 150/2180/75hp**	*Armament:* **Two 533mm (21in) TT**
Length: **39.5m (129ft 7in)**	*Surface range:* **4825km (2604nm) (estimated)**
Beam: **3.4m (11ft 2in)**	*Crew:* **19**
Draught: **4.7m (15ft 5in)**	*Launch date:* **Project cancelled**

The first operational Walter-powered boats were designated Type XVIIB. Five units were launched between 1944 and 1945 but only three, *U-1405*, *U-1406* and *U-1407*, were completed. All three were scuttled in May 1945; one of them, the *U-1407*, was salved, repaired and allocated to the Royal Navy under the name *Meteorite*. She was used to make exhaustive tests of the Walter propulsion system and was scrapped in 1950, by which time nuclear reactors were under investigation as submarine propulsion systems.

The Type XVIIBs were to have been followed by 10 Type XVIIGs, led by *U-1081*. Although the Walter turbine was their primary propulsion system, they retained diesel and electric motors to extend their overall combat radius.

The Type XVIIG class were generally similar to the Type XVIIB, although very slightly smaller. A further class of experimental boats, the Type XVIIK, was planned for the purpose of testing the closed-cycle diesel engine as an alternative to the Walter turbine, but like the XVIIG it never advanced beyond project stage.

There is little doubt that the Walter boats, had they been available two or three years earlier, would have made an enormous difference to the outcome of the Battle of the Atlantic.

U-2321

The *U-2321* was the first of the small Type XXIII electric-powered coastal submarines, which were the subject of a top-priority construction programme that took place in bomb-proof bunkers in the latter months of World War II.

Fitted with electric "creeping" motors, these Type XXIII boats were very quiet and hard to detect. Construction of this class was originally intended to go ahead at various locations, notably Hamburg, Kiel, Toulon, Genoa, Monfalcone and Nikolayev, but because of the rapid contraction of the German fronts in 1944 as the Wehrmacht suffered a series of defeats, building took place only at the German ports.

In total, 63 units were commissioned, of which 51 were either at sea or in various stages of construction when the war came to an end. The Type XXIII building programme was also seriously disrupted and delayed by Allied bombing.

The *U-2321*, commanded by Lt Barschkies, deployed to Kristiansand, Norway, and made her first war patrol off the Scottish coast in March 1945, sinking one small freighter. Together with other Type XXIIIs, she was surrendered in May 1945.

Many other Type XXIIIs, in defiance of the terms of surrender, were scuttled by their crews instead.

SPECIFICATIONS

U-2321

Displacement surfaced: **236tnes (232t)**	*Performance surfaced:* **9.75 knots**
Displacement submerged: **260tnes (256t)**	*Performance submerged:* **12.5 knots**
Powerplant: **single-shaft diesel/electric motors plus silent creeping electric motor; 580/580/35hp**	*Armament:* **two 533mm (21in) TT**
Length: **34m (112ft)**	*Surface range:* **2171km (1172nm)**
Beam: **2.9m (9ft 9in)**	*Crew:* **14**
Draught: **3.7m (12ft 3in)**	*Launch date:* **Not known**

U-2501

SPECIFICATIONS

U-2501

Displacement surfaced: **1647tnes (1621t)**	*Performance surfaced:* **15.5 knots**
Displacement submerged: **2100tnes (2067t)**	*Performance submerged:* **16 knots**
Powerplant: **twin screws, diesel/electric motors, silent creeping motors; 4000/5000/226hp at 15/15/5 knots**	*Armament:* **six 533mm (21in) TT; four 30mm AA guns**
Length: **77m (251ft 8in)**	*Surface range:* **17934km (9678nm)**
Beam: **8m (26ft 3in)**	*Crew:* **57**
Draught: **6.2m (20ft 4in)**	*Launch date:* **1944**

In 1943, with U-boats beginning to suffer serious losses, and with no prospect of the new Walter boats making an early operational debut, the German Admiralty decided on an expedient by marrying conventional submarine machinery to the new streamlined hull design.

The result was the Type XXI "electro-boat", which had a redesigned internal hull in order to provide room for more batteries, raising the underwater speed to 15 knots. The boats were fitted with "creeper" engines, for silent underwater escape at five knots.

Other innovations included a fast mechanical reloading system for the six bow torpedo tubes, a retractable Schnorchel fitted with radar warning receivers and other countermeasures devices, an electronic command centre for accurate plotting and tracking of targets, and two remotely controlled 30mm antiaircraft mountings.

The boats were ordered into mass production, with 20 units per month envisaged and an in-service target date of November 1944, but this proved totally unrealistic. In fact, the project was far too late to make a difference to the war. The *U-2501* was the first of the Type XXIs, but she never became operational, being scuttled at Hamburg on 2 May 1945.

U-2511

One of the reasons for the delay in the Type XXI becoming operational was that the boat was so radically different, and more highly capable, than anything that had preceded, and so new handling and attack techniques had to be evaluated. The other main reason was Allied bombing of Germany, which seriously disrupted the building programme.

Of the completed boats, 24 were lost through enemy action or accident. One hundred and twenty-one units were actually commissioned and 55 were deployed to Norway in March 1945 for last-ditch operations against Allied shipping in the North Sea area. Had all of the Type XXIs been used, they might have inflicted massive casualties on the Allies; as it was, their commander never received operational orders for them and an expected last stand of German forces in Norway never took place.

In fact, only two boats, *U-2511* and *U-3008*, made an operational sortie, and this was interrupted by the ending of the war. At that moment the *U-2511*'s captain had actually sighted a British cruiser, but having been advised that a German surrender was imminent, he elected to make only a dummy attack on it. *U-2511* later surrendered at Bergen and was subsequently scrapped.

SPECIFICATIONS

U-2511

Displacement surfaced: **1647tnes (1621t)**	*Performance surfaced:* **15.5 knots**
Displacement submerged: **2100tnes (2067t)**	*Performance submerged:* **16 knots**
Machinery: **twin screws, diesel/electric motors, silent creeping motors; 4000/5000/226hp at 15/15/5 knots**	*Armament:* **six 533mm (21in) TT; four 30mm AA guns**
Length: **77m (251ft 8in)**	*Surface range:* **17,934km (9678nm)**
Beam: **8m (26ft 3in)**	*Crew:* **57**
Draught: **6.2m (20ft 4in)**	*Launch date:* **1944**

CLYDE

SPECIFICATIONS

CLYDE

Displacement surfaced: **1834tnes (1805t)**	*Performance surfaced:* **21.75 knots**
Displacement submerged: **2680tnes (2723t)**	*Performance submerged:* **10 knots**
Machinery: **two screws, diesel/electric motors; 10,000/2500hp**	*Armament:* **eight 533mm (21in) TT; one 100mm (4in) gun**
Length: **99.1m (325ft)**	*Surface range:* **9265km (5000nm) at 10 knots**
Beam: **8.5m (28ft)**	*Crew:* **61**
Draught: **4.1m (13ft 6in)**	*Launch date:* **26 January 1932**

HMS *Clyde* was one of three Thames class combined fleet and patrol type submarines laid down between 1932 and 1933 and completed between 1932 and 1935. There were originally to have been 20 boats in this class, but the order was drastically reduced following a policy change. The boats featured a double hull with welded external fuel tanks, eliminating the leakage problems that had plagued earlier classes. *Clyde*, *Thames* and the third boat, *Severn*, were assigned to the 2nd Submarine Flotilla on the outbreak of World War II, beginning operations against enemy shipping in the North Sea and off the coast of Norway.

On 20 June 1940 *Clyde*, under Lt-Cdr Ingram, obtained a torpedo hit on the bow of the German battlecruiser *Gneisenau*, which had left Trondheim to make a sortie into the Iceland-Faeroes passage. The warship limped back to Trondheim and, following temporary repairs, sailed for Kiel where she remained until early 1941. This was a major success, as the German vessel was a fast and powerfully armed ship. *Clyde*'s sister boat *Thames* fell victim to a mine off Norway on 23 July 1940. After many successful forays against enemy shipping in northern waters, both boats deployed to the Eastern Fleet via the Mediterranean in 1944 and were scrapped in India in 1946.

OBERON

L aid down in 1924 at Chatham Dockyard, HM submarine *Oberon* was in many respects an experimental craft. Based on the L class, which made its appearance in the final year of World War I, she was originally designated *O1* and had a number of advanced design features, including welded fuel tanks that replaced the earlier riveted ones during the course of a refit.

Oberon had a design depth limit of 150m (500ft), but her design performances were never attained. However, she had a good radius of action, which would have made her ideal for service in Far Eastern waters, as was originally intended.

Oberon was followed into service by two more boats, *Otway* and *Oxley*, which were built by Vickers and were similar to *Oberon* except for some improvements in hull form, which were designed to give a higher speed. Both boats were laid down for the Royal Australian Navy, being returned to Britain in 1931. *Oxley* was accidentally torpedoed by HM submarine *Triton* on 10 September 1939, just 10 days after the start of World War II. *Oberon* saw war service in home waters and *Otway* in the Mediterranean. Both were broken up in 1945. The Odin class, six of which were completed in 1928, contained further improvements on the *Oberon* design.

SPECIFICATIONS

OBERON

Displacement surfaced: **1513tnes (1490t)**	*Performance surfaced:* **15.5 knots**
Displacement submerged: **1922tnes (1892t)**	*Performance submerged:* **9 knots**
Machinery: **twin screws, diesel/electric motors; 3000/1350hp**	*Armament:* **eight 533mm (21in) TT; one 100mm (4in) gun**
Length: **83.4m (273ft 8in)**	*Surface range:* **9500km (5633nm)**
Beam: **8.3m (27ft 3in)**	*Crew:* **54**
Draught: **4.6m (15ft)**	*Launch date:* **24 September 1926**

ORPHEUS

SPECIFICATIONS

ORPHEUS

Displacement surfaced:
1513tnes (1490t)

Performance surfaced:
15.5 knots

Displacement submerged:
1922tnes (1892t)

Performance submerged:
9 knots

Machinery:
**twin screws,
diesel/electric motors;
4400/1320hp**

Armament:
**eight 533mm (21in) TT;
one 100mm (4in) gun**

Length:
83.4m (273ft 8in)

Surface range:
9500km (5633nm)

Beam:
8.3m (27ft 3in)

Crew:
54

Draught:
4.6m (15ft)

Launch date:
26 February 1929

Orpheus was the last in the batch of six Odin-class submarines completed for the Royal Navy between 1929 and 1930. As with *Oberon*, the design depth limit was 150m (500ft), although operationally the boats were capable of diving to 109m (360ft). Diving trials showed that some stiffening of the hull was necessary.

Together with the class leaders, *Odin*, *Olympus* and *Otus*, *Orpheus* saw service on the East India station before being transferred to the Mediterranean Fleet in 1940, at the time of Italy's entry into World War II. Bad luck seemed to follow this class of submarine.

Odin was the first of the Odin-class boats to become a victim of enemy action. On 14 June 1940, while operating out of Malta, she was sunk in the Gulf of Taranto by the Italian destroyer *Strale*. Two more losses came in swift succession: *Orpheus* was sunk off Tobruk by the destroyer *Turbine* on 16 June 1940, while *Oswald* was sunk by the destroyer *Vivaldi* south of Calabria on 1 August 1940. A fourth boat, *Olympus*, was lost when she ran into a mine barrage during a sortie from Malta on 8 May 1942.

The two other Odin-class boats, *Osiris* and *Otus*, were both fitted with a 20mm Oerlikon gun. They survived the war and were scrapped at Durban in September 1946.

PROTEUS

The six vessels of the Parthian class, of which HM submarine *Proteus* was the sole survivor at the end of World War II, were similar to those of the Odin class, but featured an altered bow shape. All six boats in the class were laid down in 1928 and completed between 1930 and 1931. Each was fitted with Vulcan clutches and high-capacity batteries, although output was later reduced.

These Parthian-class boats were the first submarines to carry the more potent Mk VIII torpedo, which became standard armament on all subsequent British submarines of that period.

One of the boats, *Poseidon*, was lost in a collision in June 1931. At the outbreak of World War II the remaining five were on the China station, but were deployed to the Mediterranean in 1940 to help counter the threat posed by the powerful Italian fleet.

Phoenix was sunk by the Italian torpedo-boat *Albatros* off Sicily on 16 July 1940; *Perseus* was torpedoed by the Italian submarine *Enrico Toti* off Zante on 6 December 1941; *Pandora* was bombed by Italian aircraft at Malta on 1 April 1942; and *Parthian* failed to return from a sortie to the Adriatic on 11 August 1943, the probable victim of an Italian mine.

Proteus was later relegated to a training role and was broken up in 1964.

SPECIFICATIONS

PROTEUS

Displacement surfaced: **1788tnes (1760t)**	**Performance surfaced:** **17.5 knots**
Displacement submerged: **2072tnes (2040t)**	**Performance submerged:** **8.6 knots**
Machinery: **two screws,** **diesel/electric motors;** **4640/1635hp**	**Armament:** **10 533mm (21in)** **TT; one 100mm** **(3.9in) gun**
Length: **88.14m (289ft 2in)**	**Surface range:** **4262km (2300nm)** **at 7.5 knots**
Beam: **9.12m (29ft 11in)**	**Crew:** **53**
Draught: **4.85m (15ft 11in)**	**Launch date:** **23 July 1929**

SEAL

SPECIFICATIONS

SEAL

Displacement surfaced: **1524tnes (1500t)**	*Performance surfaced:* **15 knots**
Displacement submerged: **2086tnes (2053t)**	*Performance submerged:* **8.75 knots**
Machinery: **twin screws, diesel/electric motors; 3300/1630hp**	*Armament:* **six 533mm (21in) TT; one 100mm (4in) gun**
Length: **81.5m (267ft)**	*Surface range:* **10,191km (5500nm) at 10 knots**
Beam: **9m (29ft 9in)**	*Crew:* **61**
Draught: **13.75m (13ft 9in)**	*Launch date:* **7 September 1938**

In May 1940, HM submarine *Seal* achieved notoriety by becoming the first and only British submarine to be captured by the Germans.

One of six Porpoise-class boats, *Seal* had just laid a mine barrage in the southern exit of the Kattegat on 5 May 1940 when she was damaged by a mine detonation. Unable to submerge or to scuttle herself, she was forced to surrender to a German Arado 196 floatplane which appeared at first light. She was in the process of deploying to the China Station at the outbreak of war, but was ordered to return to home waters. She never reached them.

After her capture, *Seal* was designated UB in German service, and was later scuttled at Kiel on 3 May 1945.

Of the other boats in the Porpoise class, *Grampus* was sunk by the Italian torpedo-boats *Cl10* and *Circe* off Augusta on 24 June 1940; *Narwhal* failed to return from a sortie into Norwegian waters off Norway in July 1940, possibly having been sunk by a German maritime aircraft; *Cachalot* was rammed by the Italian torpedo-boat *Papa* off Cyrenaica on 4 August 1941; and *Porpoise* was sunk by Japanese air attack in the Malacca Strait on 19 January 1945. *Rorqual* survived the war, and was broken up in 1946.

SERAPH

One of 33 S-class submarines laid down under a war emergency programme initiated in 1941, *Seraph* and her sisters were improved and enlarged developments of the Shark class of the late 1930s. Though they were rushed into service, the class served the Royal Navy well during World War II.

The S class submarines, originally intended for service in the North Sea area, were offensively employed in all three main theatres of war, and proved a most successful design.

Seraph's area of operations was the Mediterranean, where, in addition to normal war patrols, she carried out many special missions, such as inserting agents along enemy coastlines – dangerous but necessary work.

During the Allied invasion of Sicily, in July 1943, *Seraph* acted as beacon submarine for Task Force 85. In July/September 1944 she was converted at Devonport to the high-speed target role, with a streamlined hull and casing, higher-capacity batteries, uprated motors and new propellers. This revised configuration increased her speed at periscope depth by some three knots.

Nine of the S class submarines were lost during World War II and two more boats, *Safari* and *Sportsman*, were lost in post-war accidents – an average loss rate compared to other classes. *Seraph* was broken up in 1965.

SPECIFICATIONS

SERAPH

Displacement surfaced: **886tnes (872t)**	*Performance surfaced:* **14.75 knots**
Displacement submerged: **1005tnes (990t)**	*Performance submerged:* **9 knots**
Machinery: **twin screws, diesel/electric motors; 1900/1300hp**	*Armament:* **six 533mm (21in) TT; one 76mm (3in) gun**
Length: **66.1m (216ft 10in)**	*Surface range:* **11,400km (6144nm)**
Beam: **7.2m (23ft 8in)**	*Crew:* **44**
Draught: **3.4m (11ft 2in)**	*Launch date:* **25 October 1941**

SPLENDID

SPECIFICATIONS

SPLENDID

Displacement surfaced: **886tnes (872t)**	Performance surfaced: **14.75 knots**
Displacement submerged: **1005tnes (990t)**	Performance submerged: **9 knots**
Machinery: **twin screws, diesel/electric motors; 1900/1300hp**	Armament: **six 533mm (21in) TT; one 76mm (3in) gun**
Length: **66.1m (216ft 10in)**	Surface range: **11,400km (6144nm)**
Beam: **7.2m (23ft 8in)**	Crew: **48**
Draught: **3.4m (11ft 2in)**	Launch date: **19 January 1942**

One of the second group of S-class submarines, *Splendid* was originally designated *P.228*. She deployed to the Mediterranean theatre, where she enjoyed some success: in November 1942, commanded by Lt-Cdr McGeogh, she torpedoed the Italian destroyer *Velite* in the Bay of Naples. In the following month she sank another Italian destroyer, the *Aviere*, as well as a 5129-tonne (5048-ton) freighter.

These successes were followed, in January 1943, by the sinking of four merchant vessels totalling 10,225 tonnes (10,064 tons), one of which was the 8058-tonne (7931-ton) *Emma*, in the Tyrrhenian Sea.

These operations by *Splendid* and other British submarines on the main convoy route between Sicily and North Africa severely disrupted Axis attempts to resupply their forces in Tunisia, which were under strong pressure from the British and American armies.

Splendid enjoyed more good fortune against enemy convoys in March 1943, when she sank four more freighters, totalling over 14,224 tonnes (14,000 tons) in the same operational area. The Germans and the Italians heavily reinforced their convoy escorts, and on 21 April 1943 *Splendid* was sunk by the German destroyer *Hermes* (the former Greek *Vasileus Georgios*) off the island of Capri.

SWORDFISH

HM submarine *Swordfish* was the second of four boats in the first group of S-class submarines. There were two groups, totalling 12 boats, and only four were to survive World War II.

Two of the boats that did not survive, *Seahorse* and *Starfish*, were lost within 48 hours of one another on 7 and 9 January 1940, the victims of German minesweepers in the Heligoland Bight.

Of the rest, *Sterlet* was sunk by German trawlers in the Skagerrak on 18 April 1940; *Shark* was also sunk by German minesweepers during a patrol off the Norwegian coast on 6 July 1940; *Salmon* was lost when she struck a mine in the same area two days later; *Spearfish* was torpedoed by *U-34* off Norway on 2 August 1940; *Swordfish* failed to return from a patrol off Ushant on 16 November 1940, possibly sunk by a mine; *Snapper* failed to return from the Bay of Biscay on 12 February 1941, the presumed victim of a mine barrage; and *Sunfish* was bombed in error by British aircraft while on passage to North Russia, having been transferred to the Soviet Navy.

Sturgeon was luckier than the others in her class: she served in home waters until 1943, when she was transferred to the Royal Netherlands Navy as the *Zeehond* (*Seadog*). She was scrapped in 1947.

SPECIFICATIONS

SWORDFISH

Displacement surfaced: **650tnes (640t)**	*Performance surfaced:* **15 knots**
Displacement submerged: **942tnes (927t)**	*Performance submerged:* **10 knots**
Machinery: **twin shafts, diesel/electric motors; 1550/1440hp**	*Armament:* **six 533mm (21in) TT; one 76mm (3in) gun**
Length: **58.8m (193ft)**	*Surface range:* **7412km (4000nm)**
Beam: **7.3m (24ft)**	*Crew:* **38**
Draught: **3.2m (10ft 6in)**	*Launch date:* **8 January 1932**

THUNDERBOLT

SPECIFICATIONS

THUNDERBOLT

Displacement surfaced: **1107tnes (1090t)**	**Performance surfaced:** **15.25 knots**
Displacement submerged: **1600tnes (1575t)**	**Performance submerged:** **9 knots**
Machinery: **twin screws,** **diesel/electric motors;** **2500/1450hp**	**Armament:** **10 533mm (21in) TT;** **one 100mm (4in) gun**
Length: **80.8m (265ft)**	**Surface range:** **7041km (3800nm)** **at 10 knots**
Beam: **8m (26ft 6in)**	**Crew:** **59**
Draught: **4.5m (14ft 9in)**	**Launch date:** **29 June 1938**

One of the first group of 15 T-class submarines, *Thunderbolt* had the dubious distinction of being lost twice during her career.

On 1 June 1939, then named HMS *Thetis*, she sank during trials with the loss of all 99 people on board. Salved and refitted, she was renamed *Thunderbolt*. On 15 December 1940, she attacked the Italian submarine *Tarantini*, which subsequently sank, in the Bay of Biscay.

Deployed to the Mediterranean, *Thunderbolt* enjoyed considerable success against Italian shipping, much of her operational time being spent in the Aegean. She also undertook some special missions, most notably on 3 January 1943, when she and another T-class boat, *Trooper*, launched Chariots (human torpedoes) in an attack on Palermo. The Chariot crews laid charges that severely damaged the Italian cruiser *Ulpio Traiano* and a large transport.

Early in 1943 *Thunderbolt* was operating in the Adriatic, where she sank several sailing vessels by gunfire. Returning to convoy attacks on the Sicily-Tunisia route, she was eventually sunk by the Italian corvette *Cicogna* on 24 March 1943.

Of the first 15 T-class submarines, a total of nine were lost in World War II.

UNBROKEN

HM submarine *Unbroken* (*P.42*) was one of the second group of U-class boats built by Vickers-Armstrong, the total output being 51 units. Four of the class were transferred on loan to the Royal Canadian Navy for training purposes and four were sent to the Far East, the remainder operating either in home waters or the Mediterranean.

On 14 August 1942, commanded by Lt Mars, *Unbroken* torpedoed the Italian cruisers *Attendolo* and *Bolzano* off the Aeolian Islands in support of Operation Pedestal, a major effort to resupply the island of Malta. From then on *Unbroken* enjoyed a very successful war career in the Mediterranean under Lt Mars and his successor, Lt Andrew.

On 26 July 1944, together with three other British submarines, *Unbroken* was handed over to the Soviet Navy and renamed as the *V-2*. The submarine remained in Soviet hands until 1949, operating from Murmansk, before returning to Britain to be scrapped in 1950.

The U-class submarines, being smaller than average in size, were able to operate very effectively in shallow coastal waters, and on the approach to harbours.

Seventeen U-class boats were lost on operations during World War II.

SPECIFICATIONS

UNBROKEN

Displacement surfaced:
  554tnes (545t)

Displacement submerged:
  752tnes (740t)

Machinery:
  twin screws,
  diesel/electric motors;
  825/615hp

Length:
  54.9m (180ft)

Beam:
  4.8m (16ft)

Draught:
  3.8m (12ft 9in)

Performance surfaced:
  11.25 knots

Performance submerged:
  9 knots

Armament:
  four 533mm (21in) TT;
  one 76mm (3in) gun

Surface range:
  7041km (3800nm)

Crew:
  31

Launch date:
  4 November 1941

UPHOLDER

SPECIFICATIONS

UPHOLDER

Displacement surfaced: **554tnes (545t)**	Performance surfaced: **11.25 knots**
Displacement submerged: **752tnes (740t)**	Performance submerged: **9 knots**
Machinery: **two screws, diesel/electric motors; 825/615hp**	Armament: **four 533mm (21in) TT; one 76mm (3in) gun**
Length: **54.9m (180ft)**	Surface range: **7041km (3800nm)**
Beam: **4.8m (16ft)**	Crew: **31**
Draught: **3.8m (12ft 9in)**	Launch date: **8 July 1940**

Another famous U-class submarine, but one that unfortunately did not survive the war, was HMS *Upholder*. Commanded by Lt-Cdr M.D. Wanklyn, she served with the Malta-based 10th Submarine Flotilla, whose boats sank 49 troops transports and supply ships totalling 152,400 tonnes (150,000 tons) from the start of June to the end of September 1941.

In May, Wanklyn was awarded the VC for sinking the Italian liner *Conte Rosso* in a particularly daring attack, and in another successful sortie on 18 September, *Upholder* sank the Italian troop-carrying liners *Neptunia* and *Oceania*, both 19,304 tonnes (19,000 tons).

On 9 November 1941 she torpedoed the Italian destroyer *Libeccio*, which sank under tow the next day, and in January 1942 she sank the Italian submarine *St Bon*, which was being used as a petrol transport.

Other successful operations against enemy convoys followed, and in March she sank the Italian submarine *Tricheco* in the central Mediterranean. Two more Italian submarines, *Guglielmotti* and *Millo*, were sunk in the same action by U-class boats *Ultimatum* and *Unbeaten*.

Upholder's phenomenal run of luck finally ran out on 14 April 1942, when she was sunk by the Italian torpedo boat *Pegaso* on her 24th war mission. She was the Royal Navy's most successful submarine.

UTMOST

Another U-class boat that started its operational career early in 1941 with the 10th Submarine Flotilla was *Utmost*, commanded by Lt-Cdr R.D. Cayley, who opened his score by sinking a freighter north of Triploi on 12 February. He sank another 5550-tonne (5463-ton) vessel on 11 February, and one of similar tonnage on 9 March.

His score continued to mount in the summer of 1941, and a close rivalry developed between the crews of *Utmost* and *Upholder*. On 28 July, *Utmost* sank a freighter of 11,629 tonnes (11,446 tons), her largest victim so far, and on the night of 1/2 November she sank the Italian freighters *Balilla* and *Marigola* in gunfire engagements on the surface. On the night of 21/22 November *Utmost* torpedoed the Italian heavy cruiser *Trieste*, which managed to reach Messina with great difficulty.

In 1942, after refitting, *Utmost* received a new captain, Lt Coombe, and in November that year she sank after being damaged by depth-charges from the Italian torpedo boat *Ardente*. In that month Allied forces carried out a successful invasion of North Africa, and from then on the Axis forces were under pressure from two sides.

The contribution made to the eventual Allied victory by Malta-based submarines like *Utmost*, which preyed on the enemy's supply lines, was massive.

SPECIFICATIONS

UTMOST

Displacement surfaced: **554tnes (545t)**	*Performance surfaced:* **11.25 knots**
Displacement submerged: **752tnes (740t)**	*Performance submerged:* **9 knots**
Machinery: **two screws, diesel/electric motors; 825/615hp**	*Armament:* **four 533mm (21in) TT; one 76mm (3in) gun**
Length: **54.9m (180ft)**	*Surface range:* **7041km (3800nm)**
Beam: **4.8m (16ft)**	*Crew:* **31**
Draught: **3.8m (12ft 9in)**	*Launch date:* **20 April 1940**

X-CRAFT

SPECIFICATIONS

X-CRAFT

Displacement surfaced: **27tnes (25.4t)**	Performance surfaced: **6.5 knots**
Displacement submerged: **30tnes (29.5t)**	Performance submerged: **5 knots**
Machinery: **single screw, diesel/electric motors; 42/30hp**	Armament: **Explosive charges**
Length: **15.7m (51ft 6in)**	Surface range: **Not recorded**
Beam: **1.8m (6ft)**	Crew: **4**
Draught: **2.6m (8ft 6in)**	Launch date: **1942**

The Royal Navy's midget submarines of World War II, known as X-craft, had their origins in a small river submarine that was being developed for the British Army by a Commander Varley in 1939.

Two prototype X-craft, the *X3* and *X4*, were built by Varley Marine, while other X and XT boats (the latter intended for training only) were produced by Vickers. Another version, designated XE, was roomier than the others and was intended for use against the Japanese in the Far East.

The X and XE craft carried side charges, each containing about two tonnes (two tons) of explosives. Designed to be placed under the bottom of the target vessel, these explosives were activated by clockwork time fuses.

The X-craft carried out some notable wartime operations, including an attack on the German battleship *Tirpitz* in Kaafjord on 23 September 1943, causing damage that effectively prevented the warship from mounting offensive operations.

In the Far East, two X-craft, *XE-1* and *XE-3*, were used to make an effective attack on the Japanese cruiser *Takao* in Singapore harbour on 30 July 1945. The warship was damaged so badly that she sank to the bottom.

ADUA

The Italian submarine *Adua* was leader of a class of 17 short-range submarines completed for the Italian Navy between 1936 and 1937, at a time when Italy and France were striving to establish naval supremacy in the Mediterranean. In fact, these two nations built more submarines in the inter-war years than any other country.

The Adua-class boats were repeats of the previous Perla class. Although not endowed with a fast surface speed, they were highly manoeuvrable and structurally strong – both considerable advantages when taking evasive action.

All of the Adua-class boats gave excellent service during World War II, although only one, the *Alagi*, survived the conflict. The rest were either destroyed in engagements with British warships or sunk by bombing.

Adua herself was sunk in the western Mediterranean (off Algeria) in a depth charge attack by the HM destroyers *Gurkha* and *Legion* on 30 September 1941.

One of the problems with the design of the Adua-class submarines was that their conning towers were too large, making them readily visible when surfaced; as a result, small conning towers were fitted to some boats during the course of the war.

Two boats, *Gondar* and *Scirè*, were equipped to carry human torpedoes.

SPECIFICATIONS

ADUA

Displacement surfaced: **691tnes (680t)**	*Performance surfaced:* **14 knots**
Displacement submerged: **880tnes (866t)**	*Performance submerged:* **7 knots**
Machinery: **two shaft, diesel/electric motors; 1200/800hp**	*Armament:* **eight 533mm (21in) TT; one 100mm (3.9in) gun**
Length: **60.2m (197ft 6in)**	*Surface range:* **18,530km (10,000nm) at 10 knots**
Beam: **6.5m (21ft 4in)**	*Crew:* **58**
Draught: **4.6mm (15ft)**	*Launch date:* **3 April 1938**

BRIN

SPECIFICATIONS

BRIN

Displacement surfaced: **1032tnes (1016t)**	Performance surfaced: **17 knots**
Displacement submerged: **1286tnes (1266t)**	Performance submerged: **8 knots**
Machinery: **two screws, diesel/electric motors; 3400/1300hp**	Armament: **eight 533mm (21in) TT; one 100mm (3.9in) gun**
Length: **70m (231ft 4in)**	Surface range: **18,530km (10,000nm) at 10 knots**
Beam: **7m (22ft 6in)**	Crew: **58**
Draught: **4.2m (13ft 6in)**	Launch date: **3 April 1938**

Derived from the Archimede class, the five Brin-class submarines were long-range boats, all launched between 1938 and 1939. Two of the boats were built in great secrecy and given the names *Archimede* and *Torricelli* to disguise the fact that two Archimede-class boats of the same name had earlier been transferred to Nationalist Spain.

Brin, named after the famous Italian naval engineer Benedetto Brin, was assigned to a submarine flotilla covering the approaches to the Aegean Sea just before Italy's entry into the war in June 1940, and in 1941 she deployed to the French Atlantic ports to take part in the Axis submarine offensive against the British Atlantic convoys. (At this period in the war, there were actually more Italian submarines than German ones operating in the Atlantic Ocean.)

After further operations in the Mediterranean, *Brin* was taken over by the Allies following the Italian armistice in September 1943 and transferred to the Royal Navy's Eastern Fleet, where she was used for anti-submarine warfare training in the Indian Ocean, though seeing no actual combat.

After performing a great deal of useful service under the Royal Navy, *Brin* was retired at the end of the war and discarded in 1948.

BARBARIGO

Completed in September 1938, *Barbarigo* was a Marcello-class submarine. She enjoyed a somewhat longer operational life than the majority of her 10n sister boats, most of which had been sunk by the end of 1942.

Barbarigo, under Cdr Ghilieri, deployed to Bordeaux in the late summer of 1940 for operations in the Central Atlantic, which began in October. The boat had no success, apart from damaging a small freighter in a surface engagement, and in January 1942 she sank a neutral Spanish ship, the *Navemar*, which was returning empty after taking Jewish refugees from Cadiz to New York.

On 6 October 1942, now under Cdr Grossi, she added farce to her record when she attacked the British corvette *Petunia*, which she mistook for an American battleship, and then claimed to have sunk her, mistaking depth-charge explosions for torpedo detonations.

A new skipper, Lt-Cdr Rigoli, finally brought a measure of success to the boat, sinking three ships on the night of 8/9 March 1943. *Barbarigo* was subsequently converted as a supply submarine for service on the France-Japan route, but was sunk by Allied aircraft in the Bay of Biscay at the start of her first trip out in June 1943.

SPECIFICATIONS

BARBARIGO

Displacement surfaced: **1059tnes (1043t)**	*Performance surfaced:* **17.4 knots**
Displacement submerged: **1310tnes (1290t)**	*Performance submerged:* **8 knots**
Machinery: **twin screws, diesel/electric motors; 3600/1100hp**	*Armament:* **eight 533mm (21in) TT**
Length: **73m (239ft 6in)**	*Surface range:* **1425km (768nm) at 10 knots**
Beam: **7m (23ft)**	*Crew:* **58**
Draught: **5m (16ft 6in)**	*Launch date:* **13 June 1938**

CAGNI

SPECIFICATIONS

CAGNI

Displacement surfaced: **1528tnes (1504t)**	*Performance surfaced:* **17 knots**
Displacement submerged: **1707tnes (1680t)**	*Performance submerged:* **9 knots**
Machinery: **twin screws, diesel/electric motors; 4370/1800hp**	*Armament:* **14 450mm (17.7in) TT; two 100mm (3.9in) guns**
Length: **87.9m (200ft 5in)**	*Surface range:* **22,236km (12,000nm) at 11 knots**
Beam: **7.76m (17ft 7in)**	*Crew:* **85**
Draught: **5.72m (13ft)**	*Launch date:* **20 July 1940**

Endowed with an exceptionally long range, the four boats of the Ammiraglio Cagni class were the biggest attack submarines ever built for the Italian Navy. They were developed specifically for commerce raiding in distant waters, and carried a large number of lesser calibre 450mm (17.7in) torpedoes for use against unarmoured merchant ships.

However, *Cagni*'s first war mission, together with her sister boat *Ammiraglio Saint-Bon*, was to transport some 305 tonnes (300 tons) of fuel and supplies from Taranto to Bardia in October 1941 in support of the Axis war effort in North Africa, evading several air attacks en route. In November 1942, under Cdr Liannazza, *Cagni* emerged from the Mediterranean, sinking one ship en route and another when she reached her war station in the South Atlantic. This first patrol lasted no less than four and a half months, an indication of *Cagni*'s excellent endurance.

During another long patrol, this time under the command of Cdr Rosselli-Lorenzini, she torpedoed the British auxiliary cruiser *Asturias* on 25 July 1943, but had no further success before the Italian surrender in September, after which she sailed into Durban.

She was the only survivor of the four boats, and was scrapped in 1948.

CALVI

One of three ocean-going boats in her class, *Pietro Calvi* was completed in October 1935. She was one of the first Italian boats to deploy to the recently captured Atlantic ports in the summer of 1940 following the fall of France, and under Cdr Caridi sank her first merchant ship in December.

A year later, having proved spectacularly unsuccessful on further Atlantic patrols, and having received a new captain, Cdr Olivieri, she was involved in a major rescue mission to pick up two sets of survivors, those of the German U-boat supply ship *Python*, which had been sunk by the British cruiser *Dorsetshire*, and those of the commerce raider *Atlantis*, sunk by the British cruiser *Devonshire*.

The rescue operation was extremely hazardous because the crews of the sunken ships had to be towed on floats by German submarines, already crammed with survivors, until the larger Italian boats could come up and take the remainder on board.

Olivieri proved to be a skilled captain. Between 25 March and 12 April 1942 he sank five ships off the coast of Brazil. On 15 July 1942, however, *Calvi* was forced to the surface while attempting to attack a convoy and sunk after a violent gun battle with British escort vessels, most notably HMS *Lulworth*.

SPECIFICATIONS

CALVI

Displacement surfaced: **1574tnes (1500t)**	Performance surfaced: **17 knots**
Displacement submerged: **2092tnes (2060t)**	Performance submerged: **8 knots**
Machinery: **twin screws, diesel/electric motors; 4400/1800**	Armament: **eight 533mm (21in) TT; two 120mm (4.7in) guns**
Length: **84.3m (276ft 6in)**	Surface range: **19,311km (10,409nm) at 10 knots**
Beam: **7.7m (25ft 3in)**	Crew: **77**
Draught: **5.2m (17ft)**	Launch date: **31 March 1935**

DANDOLO

SPECIFICATIONS

DANDOLO

Displacement surfaced: **1080tnes (1063t)**	Performance surfaced: **17.4 knots**
Displacement submerged: **1338tnes (1317t)**	Performance submerged: **8 knots**
Machinery: **two screws, diesel/electric motors; 2880/1250hp**	Armament: **eight 533mm (21in) TT; two 100mm (3.9in) guns**
Length: **73m (239ft 6in)**	Surface range: **4750km (2560nm) at 17 knots**
Beam: **7.2m (23ft 8in)**	Crew: **57**
Draught: **5m (16ft 5in)**	Launch date: **20 November 1937**

A sister vessel to *Barbarigo*, *Dandolo* was one of the nine ocean-going boats of the Marcello class, designed by the talented engineer Curio Bernardis. Her first war patrol in June 1940 was unlucky, her torpedoes just missing the new French cruiser *Jean de Vienne*.

After initial operations in the Atlantic off Madeira and the Azores, *Dandolo* (Cdr Boris) and other Italian submarines deployed to Bordeaux, from where they operated against Allied commerce in the Central Atlantic. *Dandolo* enjoyed some success, sinking one freighter of 5270 tonnes (5187 tons) and damaging another of 3828 tonnes (3768 tons). She continued to operate from Bordeaux during the winter of 1940-41, subsequently returning to Italy for a refit before recommencing operations.

Under the command of Lt-Cdr Auconi *Dandolo* sank a number of merchant ships, then acted in the role of transport submarine for a time before returning to offensive operations. On 20 July 1942, she fired a salvo of four torpedoes, all of which missed, at the aircraft carrier HMS *Eagle*. In July 1940, during the Allied invasion of Sicily, she torpedoed and damaged the British cruiser *Cleopatra*. She survived the war and was discarded in 1947.

FOCA

Completed in November 1937, *Foca* was one of three minelaying submarines, the other two being *Atropo* and *Zoea*. They were the last of such boats to be built for the Italian Navy before World War II.

On these boats the torpedo armament was sacrificed to provide two mine chutes at the stern. As originally configured, the 100mm (3.9in) gun was mounted in a shielded position in the after section of the conning tower, but this was later replaced by a gun mounted on the casing forward of the conning tower.

Foca was an early war loss; in October 1940 she sailed to lay a mine barrage off the coast of Palestine near Haifa and never returned. The theory was that she had run into a British minefield. Her two sister boats both survived the war, having surrendered at the time of the armistice in September 1943.

In November, *Atropo* and *Zoea*, together with the *Corridoni* and *Menotti*, joined the British boats *Severn* and *Rorqual* in transporting some 305 tonnes (300 tons) of supplies to the Aegean islands of Leros and Samos, which had been seized and occupied by British commandos. The Germans reacted swiftly and regained control of the islands, most of the British garrisons being captured after a fierce fight. *Atropo* and *Zoea* were both discarded in March 1947.

SPECIFICATIONS

FOCA

Displacement surfaced: **1354tnes (1333t)**	*Performance surfaced:* **15.2 knots**
Displacement submerged: **1685tnes (1659t)**	*Performance submerged:* **7.4 knots**
Machinery: **twin screws, diesel/electric motors; 2880/1250hp**	*Armament:* **six 533mm (21in) TT; one 100mm (3.9in) gun**
Length: **82.8m (271ft 8in)**	*Surface range:* **4632nm (2500nm) at 17 knots**
Beam: **7.2m (23ft 6in)**	*Crew:* **60**
Draught: **5.3m (17ft 5in)**	*Launch date:* **26 June 1937**

FLUTTO

SPECIFICATIONS

FLUTTO

Displacement surfaced: **973tnes (958t)**	Performance surfaced: **16 knots**
Displacement submerged: **1189tnes (1170t)**	Performance submerged: **7 knots**
Machinery: **twin screws, diesel/electric motors**	Armament: **six 533mm (21in) TT**
Length: **63.2m (207ft)**	Surface range: **5297km (3200nm)**
Beam: **7m (23ft)**	Crew: **50**
Draught: **4.9m (16ft)**	Launch date: **November 1942**

The *Flutto* was the class leader of the first of three planned groups of submarines that would have reached a total of 49 boats, all embodying the lessons absorbed by the Italian Navy since it entered the war in June 1940. The plan called for production to be completed by the end of 1944; in the event, production was overtaken by the armistice of September 1943, and only a few of the first group, including class leader *Flutto*, ever saw active military service.

Two of the class, *Grongo* and *Murena*, were fitted with cylinders for transporting human torpedoes. *Flutto* was sunk by Royal Navy MTBs *640*, *651* and *670* in the Straits of Messina on 11 July 1943, during the Allied invasion of Sicily, Operation Husky.

Of her sister boats, *Gorgo* was sunk by the American destroyer USS *Nields* off Algeria on 21 May 1943, and *Tritone* was sunk by gunfire from the British destroyer *Antelope* and the Canadian corvette *Port Arthur* off Bougie on 19 January 1943.

Other boats in the class were sunk in harbour after being seized by the Germans or destroyed in various stages of construction by Allied air attacks. One, the *Nautilo*, was refloated and handed over to the Yugoslav Navy as the *Sava*; the *Murea* went to the USSR in 1949, designated the *Z13*.

GALILEI

Assigned to the Nationalist forces during the Spanish Civil War, the Archimede-class submarine *Galileo Galilei* gave the Italian Navy much valuable experience of operational patrolling in a war zone, an experience shared by her sister boat, *Galileo Ferraris*.

The class leader, *Archimede*, was secretly transferred to Spain in 1937, together with the *Evangelista Torricelli*, the boats being respectively named *General Sanjurjo* and *General Mola*.

Italy's entry into the war on the Axis side in June 1940 found *Galilei* and *Ferraris* at their war stations in the Red Sea, *Ferraris* making an unsuccessful attempt to attack the British battleship *Royal Sovereign*, which was passing through the Suez Canal.

On 10 October, *Galilei* engaged the British armed trawler *Moonstone*, whose accurate gunfire killed nearly all the submarine's officers and damaged the air-conditioning system, which emitted toxic fumes and asphyxiated those crew members inside the boat. Floating on the sea, *Galilei* was taken into Royal Navy service as training boat *X2*, with the pennant number *P.711*. She was discarded in 1946.

Her sister boat *Ferraris* was caught on the surface and sunk by air attack and gunfire in the North Atlantic on 25 October 1941.

SPECIFICATIONS

GALILEI

Displacement surfaced: **1000tnes (985t)**	Performance surfaced: **17 knots**
Displacement submerged: **1279tnes (1259t)**	Performance submerged: **8.5 knots**
Machinery: **twin screws, diesel/electric motors; 3000/1300hp**	Armament: **eight 533mm (21in) TT; two 100mm (3.9in) guns**
Length: **70.5m (231ft 4in)**	Surface range: **6670km (3600nm)**
Beam: **6.8m (22ft 4in)**	Crew: **55**
Draught: **4m (13ft 5in)**	Launch date: **19 March 1934**

MAMELI

SPECIFICATIONS

MAMELI

Displacement surfaced: **843tnes (830t)**	*Performance surfaced:* **17 knots**
Displacement submerged: **1026tnes (1010t)**	*Performance submerged:* **7 knots**
Machinery: **twin screws, diesel/electric motors; 3000/1100hp**	*Armament:* **six 533mm (21in) TT; one 102mm (4in) gun**
Length: **64.6m (212ft)**	*Surface range:* **5930km (3200nm) at 10 knots**
Beam: **6.5m (21ft 4in)**	*Crew:* **49**
Draught: **4.3m (14ft)**	*Launch date:* **9 December 1926**

The four Mameli-class submarines were, in effect, prototypes for several of the Italian Navy's subsequent ocean-going submarine designs, and were the first of their type to come into service after World War I, during which Italy had fought Germany.

The design of the Mameli-class boats incorporated much that had been learned from an appraisal of captured German U-boats, and the Mameli class were able to reach diving depths that had not previously been possible with Italian boats.

Goffredo Mameli (previously named *Masaniello*) and two of her sister boats, *Giovanni Procida* and *Tito Speri*, all survived World War II and were discarded in 1948. The fourth boat, *Pier Capponi*, was torpedoed by HM submarine *Rorqual* south of Stromboli on 31 March 1941.

All four submarines saw active service in support of Nationalist forces during the Spanish Civil War. *Mameli*, under Cdr Maiorana, had an early success in the weeks after Italy entered the war, sinking a freighter between Alexandria and Crete, but apart from that she had a particularly undistinguished war. As with other Italian submarines of this period, the large surface area of her conning tower proved an excellent target and hence a disadvantage.

PERLA

O ne of 10 submarines in her class, all completed in
1936, *Perla* was on patrol in the Indian Ocean when
Italy entered the war. Under Lt-Cdr Napp, she remained
there until early March 1941, when she departed
Massawa and sailed for Bordeaux via the Cape of Good
Hope, being replenished en route by the German
commerce raider *Atlantis*. With *Perla* went the other
Italian submarines *Archimede*, *Guglielmotti* and *Ferraris*.

By the spring of 1942 *Perla* was back in the
Mediterranean, attacking Royal Navy Malta convoys and
seeking targets in the waters around Cyprus. This
part of the eastern Mediterranean was rich in oil-tanker
traffic, which regularly plied its trade between Syrian
ports and Egypt.

It was while carrying out these activities, on 9 July
1942, that *Perla* was forced to the surface and captured
off Beirut by the British corvette *Hyacinth*.

She was eventually handed over to the Royal Hellenic
Navy and renamed *Matrozos*, serving on patrol duty
around the islands in the Aegean until the end of World
War II. She was scrapped in 1954.

Two of the Perla-class boats, *Iride* and *Ambra*,
were fitted with canisters for the carriage of human
torpedoes. Five of this class were lost by the Italian Navy
during World War II.

SPECIFICATIONS

PERLA

Displacement surfaced: **707tnes (696t)**	*Performance surfaced:* **14 knots**
Displacement submerged: **865tnes (852t)**	*Performance submerged:* **8 knots**
Machinery: **two screws, diesel/electric motors; 1400/800hp**	*Armament:* **six 533mm (21in) TT; one 100mm (3.9in) gun**
Length: **60m (196ft 9in)**	*Surface range:* **6670km (3595nm) at 10 knots**
Beam: **6.5m (21ft 2in)**	*Crew:* **45**
Draught: **5m (15ft 3in)**	*Launch date:* **3 May 1936**

SQUALO

SPECIFICATIONS

SQUALO

Displacement surfaced: **948tnes (933t)**	Performance surfaced: **15 knots**
Displacement submerged: **1160tnes (1142t)**	Performance submerged: **8 knots**
Machinery: **two diesel/ electric motors; 3000/1300hp**	Armament: **eight 533mm (21in) TT; one 102mm (4in) gun**
Length: **70m (229ft)**	Surface range: **7412km (4000nm) at 10 knots**
Beam: **7m (23ft 7in)**	Crew: **52**
Draught: **7m (23ft 7in)**	Launch date: **15 January 1930**

The leader of a class of four submarines, *Squalo* was on patrol in the eastern Mediterranean when Italy declared war on the Allies, covering an area from the Aegean to the Levant.

Apart from accounting for a few small sailing craft, sunk by gunfire on the surface (nearly all World War II submarines, of whatever navy, were designed to attack their targets on the surface), her operations were unsuccessful; this was mainly due to the fact that Italian naval intelligence on the movements of British shipping was almost always defective, and submarines were ordered to patrol the wrong areas.

Other Squalo-class boats, however, enjoyed more success. On July 1941, for example, *Delfino* shot down the RAF *Sunderland* flying boat that was attacking her and took four of its crew prisoner. Such instances were comparatively rare, but not unknown during air-sea warfare in World War II.

Delfino was accidentally sunk in a collision in 1943. Of the other two boats, *Narvalo* was scuttled after being damaged by British destroyers off Tripoli in January 1943, while *Tricheco* was sunk by HM submarine *Upholder* off Brindisi in March 1942.

Squalo was discarded in 1948, having been laid up before Italy's armistice with the Allies.

I-7

The J3 class submarine *I-7* and her sister boat, *I-8*, were among the first submarines of pure Japanese design and, at the time of their commissioning, were the largest in the Imperial Japanese Navy. They would begin a trend for large submarines in the Japanese Navy, a trend that was to prove utterly futile in serving Japan's wartime needs. Large submarines used lots of fuel and had short endurance at sea.

Approved in the 1934 naval construction programme, their design was based on a submarine cruiser concept, developed from the earlier KD3 and KD4 designs, and they had provision for a Yokosuka E14Y1 reconnaissance seaplane (codenamed Glen by the Allies).

The aircraft made its operational debut on 17 December 1941, when *I-7* launched its Glen on a dawn reconnaissance over Pearl Harbor to assess the damage done by carrier-based attack aircraft. *I-7* had an endurance of 60 days and a respectable diving depth of 99m (325ft).

I-7 and her sister sank seven Allied merchant vessels, totalling 42,574 tonnes (41,902 tons) during the course of the Pacific war. *I-7* was sunk by the American destroyer *Monaghan* off the Aleutian islands on 22 June 1943, while *I-8* was sunk by the destroyers USS *Morrison* and *Stockton* off Okinawa on 30 March 1945.

SPECIFICATIONS

I-7

Displacement surfaced: **2565tnes (2525t)**	*Performance surfaced:* **23 knots**
Displacement submerged: **3640tnes (3583t)**	*Performance submerged:* **8 knots**
Machinery: **twin screws, diesel/electric motors; 11,200/2800hp**	*Armament:* **six 533mm (21in) TT; one 140mm (5.5in) gun**
Length: **109.3m (358ft 7in)**	*Surface range:* **26,600km (14,337nm) at 16 knots**
Beam: **9m (29ft 6in)**	*Crew:* **100**
Draught: **5.2m (17ft)**	*Launch date:* **3 July 1935**

I-15

SPECIFICATIONS

I-15

Displacement surfaced: **2625tnes (2584t)**	*Performance surfaced:* **23.5 knots**
Displacement submerged: **3713tnes (3654t)**	*Performance submerged:* **8 knots**
Machinery: **two screws, diesel/electric motors; 12,400/2000hp**	*Armament:* **six 533mm (21in) TT; one 140mm (5.5in) and two 25mm AA guns**
Length: **102.5m (336ft)**	*Surface range:* **29,648km (16,000nm)**
Beam: **9.3m (30ft 6in)**	*Crew:* **100**
Draught: **5.1m (16ft 9in)**	*Launch date:* **7 March 1939**

Developed from the earlier KD6-class cruiser-type submarines, the I-15 class were designed for long-range scouting. Like the I-7 class, they were equipped with a Yokosuka E14Y1 Glen reconnaissance seaplane, which on one occasion was used as a bomber aircraft.

In 1942, a Glen flown by Warrant Officer Fujita was launched from the I-15-class submarine *I-25*, which was cruising off the US west coast. The aircraft carried four 76kg (168lb) incendiary bombs in place of its observer, and these were dropped in a forested area of Oregon, causing limited damage. It was the first and only time that the continental United States was attacked by an enemy aircraft.

The I-15-class boats saw extensive war service, one of their missions being to run supplies and diplomatic personnel to and from Japan and the French Atlantic ports. On 15 October 1942 *I-15* and her sister boat *I-19* took part in a highly successful attack on the aircraft carrier USS *Wasp*, which was hit by *I-19* and had to be abandoned, and the destroyer *O'Brien*, which was torpedoed by *I-15* and sank four days later.

On 27 October *I-15* narrowly missed the battleship *Washington*. The submarine was herself sunk on 2 November 1942.

I-16

Ordered in 1937, the five boats of the I-16 class were the first Japanese submarines to be laid down in the scramble for naval expansion that followed the expiry of the London Naval Treaty.

Optimized for attack, they carried a heavy armament and had an endurance of 90 days. Prior to the attack on Pearl Harbor the five submarines (*I-16*, *I-18*, *I-20*, *I-22* and *I-24*) each loaded a Type A midget submarine on a fitting abaft the conning tower and launched them off the US naval base on the night of 6/7 December 1941. All the midgets were unsuccessful, however.

One of the midget craft was sunk by the destroyer USS *Ward* in the first action of the Pacific War, two were sunk penetrating the harbour and the other two in the harbour itself before they could launch their torpedoes at their targets.

At the beginning of 1943, *I-16* was modified as a transport submarine, with provision for a Daihatsu landing craft and other equipment for supplying Japanese troops on beleaguered islands. On 14 May 1944, while on just such a transport mission to the Solomons, *I-16* was located by a US destroyer escort group and sunk by a "hedgehog" salvo.

The other four boats were also sunk during the war, all between 1942 and 1943.

SPECIFICATIONS

I-16

Displacement surfaced: **2595tnes (2554t)**	**Performance surfaced:** **23.6 knots**
Displacement submerged: **3618tnes (3561t)**	**Performance submerged:** **8 knots**
Machinery: **two screws,** **diesel/electric motors;** **12,400/2000hp**	**Armament:** **eight 533mm (21in) TT;** **one 140mm (5.5in)** **and two 25mm AA guns**
Length: **103.80m (340ft 7in)**	**Surface range:** **25,942km (14,000nm)**
Beam: **9.10m (29ft 10in)**	**Crew:** **100**
Draught: **5.35m (17ft 7in)**	**Launch date:** **28 July 1938**

I-52

SPECIFICATIONS

I-52

Displacement surfaced: **2605tnes (2564t)**	Performance surfaced: **17.7 knots**
Displacement submerged: **3618tnes (3561t)**	Performance submerged: **6.5 knots**
Machinery: **two screws, diesel/electric motors; 4700/1200hp**	Armament: **six 533mm (21in) TT; two 140mm (5.5in) and two 25mm AA guns**
Length: **102.4m (335ft 11in)**	Surface range: **38,913km (21,000nm) at 16 knots**
Beam: **9.3m (30ft 6in)**	Crew: **101**
Draught: **5.12m (16ft 10in)**	Launch date: **1943**

The five I-52 class (Type C3) submarines were authorized in 1942 under the Japanese 1941–42 War Programme, but only three were built.

The I-52 class submarines were generally similar to those of the preceding I-16 (C2) class, except that they carried a reduced number of torpedoes and less powerful diesel engines, the higher-powered units at that time being in short supply. The reduction in weight and increase in space meant that extra fuel could be carried, greatly enhancing the operational radius of these boats. However, even with greater range these vessels were still vulnerable to roving Allied aircraft.

I-52 herself was modified as a transport submarine, embarking on her first voyage to Europe via the Indian Ocean in May 1944. On the night of 23/24 June, having made rendezvous with the German *U-530* to take on board specialist search radar equipment, she was sunk near the Azores by Grumman Avenger aircraft from the carrier USS *Bogue*, the Avengers fixing her position with the help of sonobuoys, recently developed in the United States of America.

Of the other two boats, *I-53* was converted to a Kaiten midget submarine carrier and survived the war, being scuttled by the United States Navy in 1946, while *I-55* was sunk by US forces off Tinian on 28 July 1944.

I-58

The *I-58* was one of three Type B3 submarines that were completed between March and September 1944. *I-56* and *I-58* were converted to Kaiten midget submarine carriers, and in January 1945, together with other similarly equipped submarines, they took part in Operation Kongo, in which attempted attacks were made on US naval bases.

The missions by *I-56* and *I-58*, against Manus in the Admiralty Islands and by *I-58* on Apra Harbour on Guam, were unsuccessful. Similar operations in opposition to the American landings on the island of Iwo Jima also proved abortive, but on the night of 27/28 July the submarine, under Cdr Hashimoto, launched a Kaiten and probably damaged the destroyer USS *Lowry*.

The action that assured *I-58* a place in naval history, however, occurred on the night of 29/30 July, when she launched a salvo of six torpedoes at the unescorted heavy cruiser USS *Indianapolis* (Capt McVay) east of Luzon. The cruiser was making for Leyte at speed after delivering parts of atomic bombs from San Francisco to Tinian, from where the fateful missions against Hiroshima and Nagasaki were flown. Of the cruiser's crew of 1199 only 316 survived. *I-58* was scuttled by the US Navy in April 1946.

SPECIFICATIONS

I-58

Displacement surfaced: 2605tnes (2564t)	**Performance surfaced:** 17.7 knots
Displacement submerged: 3618tnes (3561t)	**Performance submerged:** 6.5 knots
Machinery: two screws, diesel/electric motors; 4700/1200hp	**Armament:** six 533mm (21in) TT; two 140mm (5.5in) and two 25mm AA guns
Length: 102.40m (335ft 11in)	**Surface range:** 38,913km (21,000nm) at 16 knots
Beam: 9.30m (30ft 6in)	**Crew:** 101
Draught: 5.12m (16ft 10in)	**Launch date:** 1944

KAITEN

SPECIFICATIONS

KAITEN

Displacement surfaced: **unknown**	Performance surfaced: **30 knots maximum**
Displacement submerged: **8.6tnes (8.5t)**	Performance submerged: **unknown**
Machinery: **one 550hp petrol- oxygen engine**	Armament: **one 1550kg (3416lb) HE warhead**
Length: **14.73m (48ft)**	Surface range: **92km (50nm) at 12 knots/25km (14nm) at 30 knots**
Beam: **0.99m (3ft 4in)**	Crew: **1**
Draught: **3.61m (3ft 3in)**	Launch date: **1944–45**

The Kaiten midget submarines, deployed in the closing months of World War II, were the Imperial Japanese Navy's equivalent of the Kamikaze suicide aircraft. They were built onto the body of a Type 93 torpedo engine and air chamber, and early models were provided with a small hatch under the hull to enable the pilot to escape as soon as the craft was locked on to its target. This escape facility was later removed, and the Kaiten became a true suicide weapon.

The *Kaiten 1* was powered by petrol and oxygen. The next version, the *Kaiten 2*, was powered by a hydrogen peroxide engine, but only a few examples were built as insufficient engines of this type were available. As a consequence, a *Kaiten 4* was built, using the conventional petrol and oxygen engine and carrying a heavier warhead to ensure penetration of enemy hulls.

The *Kaiten 3* was an experimental unit which never entered production. The *Kaiten 2* and *4* carried a two-man crew. Hundreds of Kaiten were built, and were intended to be used primarily for coastal defence in opposition to the expected invasion of Japan, although many were deployed against Allied naval forces elsewhere and were first used in the battle for the Philippines, November 1944. The specifications table at left is for the *Kaiten 1*.

I-121

The four I-121-class (Type KRS) submarines were developed from the former German *U-125*, which had been surrendered to Japan after World War I, and were virtually identical in performance, size and appearance. All four were intended specifically for minelaying, and could carry 42 mines in addition to their complement of torpedoes.

On the night of 6/7 December 1941, just prior to the attack on Pearl Harbor, *I-121* (Cdr Yendo) and *I-122* (Cdr Utsuki) laid mine barrages off the north-east exits from Singapore. The same two boats sowed more mines off Singapore between 8 and 15 December, while their sister submarines *I-123* (Cdr Ueno) and *I-124* (Cdr Kishigami) carried out similar operations off the Philippines, the latter boat also sinking a ship with her four torpedoes.

Later in December all four boats were involved in minelaying in Indonesian waters, and in January 1942 they were in Australian waters, *I-124* being sunk off Port Darwin on the 20th.

In the summer of 1942 the remaining boats acted as tankers for fleet reconnaissance aircraft off the Hawaiian Islands. During the battle off the Solomon Islands in August, *I-121* was damaged by carrier aircraft and later relegated to the training role. She was scrapped in 1946.

SPECIFICATIONS

I-121

Displacement surfaced: 1405tnes (1383t)	**Performance surfaced:** 14.5 knots
Displacement submerged: 1796tnes (1768t)	**Performance submerged:** 7 knots
Machinery: two screws, diesel/electric motors; 2400/1100hp	**Armament:** four 533mm (21in) TT; one 140mm (5.5in) gun, two mines
Length: 82m (269ft)	**Surface range:** 19,456km (10,500nm) at 8 knots
Beam: 7.52m (24ft 8in)	**Crew:** 75
Draught: 4.42m (14ft 6in)	**Launch date:** unknown

I-153

SPECIFICATIONS

I-153

Displacement surfaced: **1828tnes (1800t)**	*Performance surfaced:* **20 knots**
Displacement submerged: **2337tnes (2300t)**	*Performance submerged:* **8 knots**
Machinery: **two screws, diesel/electric motors; 6800/1800hp**	*Armament:* **eight 533mm (21in) TT; one 105mm (4.7in) gun**
Length: **94.49m (310ft)**	*Surface range:* **18,530km (10,000nm) at 8 knots**
Beam: **7.98m (26ft 2in)**	*Crew:* **60**
Draught: **4.83m (15ft 10in)**	*Launch date:* **5 August 1925**

The *I-153* was one of four Type KD3a boats approved in the extensive 1923–28 Japanese naval building programme and completed between March and December 1927.

Originally designated *No 64*, she later became *I-53*; two other boats were designated *No 77* (*I-54*) and *No 78* (*I-55*) respectively. The fourth boat, *I-58*, did not have a prior number and is sometimes classed as a Type KD3b.

All the surviving boats were renumbered in May 1942, *I-53* becoming *I-153* and so on. Before that, *I-53* was active in the waters around the Dutch East Indies archipelago, attacking ships evacuating Allied personnel from Java. During these operations, *I-53*, under Cdr Nakamura, sank three ships totalling 11,178 tonnes (11,002 tons).

During the Pacific war, submarines of the KD3a and KD3b classes, nine boats in all, sank 17 Allied ships totalling 63,380 tonnes (62,379 tons). By the summer of 1942 all submarines in this class had been relegated to the training role, although some were later reinstated as Kaiten carriers.

I-153 and *I-154* were disarmed in 1944 and surrendered at the end of the war, being scrapped by the Americans in 1946.

I-201

The I-201 class of very advanced submarines owed its origin to an experimental submarine from 1937, known as *No 71*. Endowed with a very streamlined hull, *No 71* attained a remarkably high underwater speed of 21.75 knots, even though on average her electric motors produced only 1800hp.

No 71 was scrapped in 1940, after she had been exhaustively tested, and much of the data she yielded was incorporated in the *I-201* and her sister boats, ordered under an emergency war construction programme between 1943 and 1944, when Japan was losing heavily.

The *I-201* compared very favourably with the German Type XXI and in fact used lightweight MAN diesels of German origin, coupled with 5000hp electric motors that gave an impressive underwater speed of 19 knots, which could be maintained for nearly an hour. The boats had an endurance of 25 days and had a diving depth of 108m (355ft), deeper than any other Japanese submarine, but to no avail.

None of the I-201 (Type ST) class ever carried out a war patrol, most of the boats, including *I-201*, being scuttled by the US Navy after the end of the war. Only *I-204* was lost to enemy action, being sunk in an air attack at Kure on 22 June 1945 when almost complete and ready for sea.

SPECIFICATIONS

I-201

Displacement surfaced: **1311tnes (1291t)**	Performance surfaced: **15.7 knots**
Displacement submerged: **1473tnes (1450t)**	Performance submerged: **19 knots**
Machinery: **twin screws, diesel/electric motors; 2750/5000hp**	Armament: **four 533mm (21in) TT; two 25mm AA guns**
Length: **79m (259ft 2in)**	Surface range: **10,747km (5800nm) at 14 knots**
Beam: **5.8m (19ft)**	Crew: **100**
Draught: **5.4m (17ft 9in)**	Launch date: **1944**

I-351

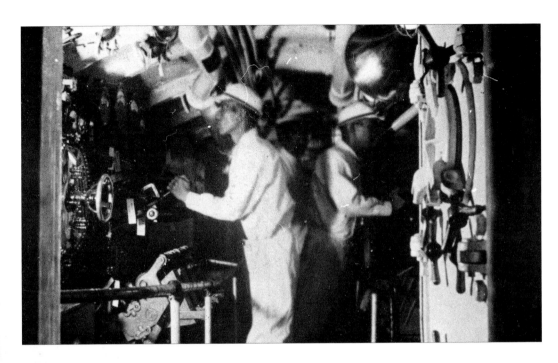

SPECIFICATIONS

I-351

Displacement surfaced: **3568tnes (3512t)**	*Performance surfaced:* **15.7 knots**
Displacement submerged: **4358tnes (4290t)**	*Performance submerged:* **19 knots**
Machinery: **twin screws, diesel/electric motors**	*Armament:* **four 533mm (12in) TT**
Length: **110m (361ft)**	*Surface range:* **24,089km (13,000nm)**
Beam: **10.2m (33ft 6in)**	*Crew:* **90**
Draught: **6m (20ft)**	*Launch date:* **1944**

In 1941, the Japanese Admiralty foresaw that both flying boats and seaplanes would have a major part to play in a war that encompassed the vast expanse of the Pacific, particularly from the aerial reconnaissance point of view, and that these aircraft were not always likely to have the benefit of shore-based facilities – a basically sound theory.

A requirement was therefore formulated for a class of three submarines (Type SH) configured as mobile supply bases, equipped to carry 396 tonnes (390 tons) of cargo, including 371 tonnes (365 tons) of petrol, 11 tonnes (11 tons) of fresh water and 60 250kg (550lb) bombs, or alternatively 30 bombs and 15 aircraft torpedoes (the Germans used similar supply vessels).

Only one boat, the *I-351*, was completed and the third (*I-353*) was cancelled in 1943.

The *I-351*'s operational career was shortlived. On 14 July 1945 she was torpedoed and sunk by the American submarine USS *Bluefish* (Lt-Cdr Forbes) while operating in the area of Southeast Asia. The second boat, *I-352*, was 90 per cent complete when she was destroyed in an air attack on Kure.

The boats of this class had a safe diving depth of 96m (315ft) and had an underwater range of 185km (100nm) at three knots.

I-400

In 1942, at the instigation of Imperial Japanese Navy Commander-in-Chief Admiral Isoroku Yamamoto, the Navy Planning Staff investigated the feasibility of mounting a torpedo attack on the locks of the Panama Canal, using aircraft launched from a submarine.

Yamamoto pressed a reluctant Imperial HQ to go ahead with the building of 19 very large submarines capable of carrying two or three aircraft, and the result was the *I-400* Type STo.

In the event, only two submarines, *I-400* and *I-401*, were completed as aircraft carriers, being fitted with a large aircraft hangar offset to starboard. The hangar could accommodate three Aichi M6A1 Seiran floatplanes, plus components for a fourth. To launch the aircraft, the submarine would surface, then the machines would be warmed up in the hangar before being rolled out, their wings unfolded, and launched down a 26m (85ft) catapult rail.

The Panama mission, which was never a viable option for the Japanese Navy, was never flown, and the two boats were surrendered in 1945 and scrapped by the US Navy in 1946. Also scrapped by the USN was *I-402*, completed on the stocks as a submarine tanker/transport. Another boat, *I-404*, was almost complete when she was sunk at her moorings in an air raid.

SPECIFICATIONS

I-400

Displacement surfaced: **5316tnes (5233t)**	*Performance surfaced:* **18.7 knots**
Displacement submerged: **6665tnes (6560t)**	*Performance submerged:* **6.5 knots**
Machinery: **twin screws, diesel/electric motors; 7700/2400hp**	*Armament:* **eight 533mm (21in) TT; one 140mm (5.5in) gun**
Length: **116m (380ft 7in)**	*Surface range:* **68,561km (37,000nm) at 14 knots**
Beam: **12m (39ft 4in)**	*Crew:* **100**
Draught: **7m (23ft)**	*Launch date:* **1944**

RO-100

SPECIFICATIONS

RO-100

Displacement surfaced: **611tnes (601t)**	Performance surfaced: **14 knots**
Displacement submerged: **795tnes (782t)**	Performance submerged: **8 knots**
Machinery: **twin screws, diesel/electric motors; 1100/760hp**	Armament: **four 533mm (21in) TT; one 76mm (3in) gun**
Length: **57.4m (188ft 3in)**	Surface range: **6485km (3500nm) at 12 knots**
Beam: **6.1m (20ft)**	Crew: **75**
Draught: **3.5m (11ft 6in)**	Launch date: **6 December 1941**

Ordered under the Japanese Navy's 1940 and 1941 programmes, the 18 Ro-100 (Type KS) small, medium-class submarines were intended for use in coastal waters, within easy reach of their operational bases. Because of this they had an operational endurance of only three weeks. Submerged range was 111km (60nm) at 3 knots and they had a diving depth of 75m (245ft).

The class enjoyed some success during the Pacific war, sinking six merchant ships totalling 35,247 tonnes (34,690 tons) and damaging three more totalling 14,300 tonnes (14,074 tons). In addition, *Ro-106* (Lt Nakamura) sank the tank landing ship *LST 342* off New Georgia on 18 July 1943, while *Ro-108* sank the US destroyer *Henley* off Finschhafen (New Guinea) on 3 October 1943.

All 18 boats became war losses. *Ro-100*'s operational career began in January 1943, when she operated in the area of the Solomons and off New Guinea. She was sunk on 25 November 1943 while carrying out a transport mission in support of operations in the New Hebrides.

Five other boats of the Ro-100 class were sunk in a period of only eight days in May 1944 by the escort destroyer USS *England*.

JASTRZAB

The *Jastrzab* (Hawk) was the former American submarine *S25*, which had been scheduled for delivery to the Royal Navy for trials to assess the possible usefulness of the older US S- and R-class boats by the British. Instead, for propaganda reasons, she was commissioned in 1941 as the Polish *Jastrzab*, flying the White Ensign of the RN as well as the flag of Poland and carrying the pennant number *P.551* (Poland had been overrun in 1939).

Jastrzab was manned by the crew of the Polish submarine *Wilk*. Despite the fact that all S-class boats assigned to the RN were relegated to training duties, *Jastrzab*'s crew insisted on being sent into action, and at the end of April 1942 she was deployed as part of the screening force for the Russian convoy PQ.15, a highly hazardous mission.

On 2 May, having departed from her assigned station, she was attacked and sunk in error by the Norwegian destroyer *St Albans* and the British minesweeper *Seagull* in the Norwegian Sea.

Jastrzab/*S25* was one of six S-class boats allocated to the Royal Navy. They were mostly used for training. Of the others, *P.553* and *P.554* were loaned to the Royal Canadian Navy, while *P.552* served in the Eastern Fleet and the South Atlantic.

SPECIFICATIONS

JASTRZAB

Displacement surfaced: 864tnes (850t)	**Performance surfaced:** 14.5 knots
Displacement submerged: 1107tnes (1090t)	**Performance submerged:** 11 knots
Machinery: two screws, diesel/electric motors; 1200/1500hp	**Armament:** four 533mm (21in) TT; one 102mm (4in) gun
Length: 64.3m (211ft)	**Surface range:** 7782km (4200nm)
Beam: 6.25m (20ft 6in)	**Crew:** 42
Draught: 4.6m (15ft 3in)	**Launch date:** 29 May 1922

ORZEL

SPECIFICATIONS

ORZEL

Displacement surfaced: **1117tnes (1100t)**	*Performance surfaced:* **15 knots**
Displacement submerged: **1496tnes (1473t)**	*Performance submerged:* **8 knots**
Machinery: **twin screws, diesel/electric motors; 4740/1100hp**	*Armament:* **12 550mm (21.7in) TT; one 105mm (4in) gun**
Length: **84m (275ft 7in)**	*Surface range:* **13,300km (7169nm) at 10 knots**
Beam: **6.7m (22ft)**	*Crew:* **56**
Draught: **4m (13ft 8in)**	*Launch date:* **15 January 1938**

Commissioned on 2 February 1939, the large ocean-going Polish submarine *Orzel* (Eagle) was built with funds raised by public subscription. She was built in Holland at De Schelde Navy Yard, Vlissingen; her sister boat, *Sep*, was built at Rotterdam Dockyard. The latter boat was still in Rotterdam in April 1939 and sailed for Gdynia before her builders' trials were completed in order to escape possible German sabotage following the invasion of Czechoslovakia.

Both boats put to sea when Germany attacked Poland at the beginning of September, *Sep* being interned at Stavnas, Sweden, on 17 September 1939; *Orzel* was likewise interned at Tallin on 15 September, some of her equipment being confiscated.

Despite the odds against him, *Orzel*'s commander, Lt-Cdr Grudzinski, broke out and made for the British Isles, arriving at Rosyth, Scotland, on 14 October, after a dangerous voyage through minefields without charts (which had been confiscated in Estonia) and evading German air and sea patrols.

Operating with the Royal Navy, *Orzel* sank two large enemy troop transports off Norway on 8 April 1940, but failed to return from a patrol in June, and was presumed to have been sunk by a mine. *Sep* was returned to Poland in 1945 and discarded in 1946.

WILK

The *Wilk* (Wolf) and her two sister boats, *Rys* and *Zbik*, were French-built minelaying submarines of the Normand-Fenaux type, ordered in 1926. Basically enlarged versions of the French Saphir class, they were good seaworthy boats but had the major disadvantage of being noisy. Also, their external fuel tanks were prone to leakages and their minelaying system was totally unreliable.

When Germany invaded Poland in September 1939 *Rys* and *Zbik* were both interned in Sweden; they were returned to Poland in 1945 and served for several years in the Polish Navy. *Wilk* was damaged by depth-charges on 2 September 1939, but despite this managed to escape to Britain through the Sund Narrows, reaching Rosyth on 20 September. In June 1940, en route to Norwegian waters, she attacked and sank the Dutch submarine *O13* in error.

She was used as a training boat from September 1940, but because of her poor condition was decommissioned in April 1942. She was towed to Poland in 1951 and later scrapped. Two British U-class submarines, *Urchin* and *P52*, also served under the Polish flag in World War II, as the *Sokol* (Falcon) and *Dzik* (Beast). They gave excellent service in the Mediterranean, where they were known as the "Terrible Twins".

SPECIFICATIONS

WILK

Displacement surfaced: 996tnes (980t)	**Performance surfaced:** 14 knots
Displacement submerged: 1270tnes (1250t)	**Performance submerged:** 9 knots
Machinery: two screws, diesel/electric motors; 1800/1200hp	**Armament:** six 550mm (21.5in) TT; one 100mm (3.9in) gun; 40 mines
Length: 78.5m (257ft 6in)	**Surface range:** 4632km (2500nm)
Beam: 5.9m (19ft 4in)	**Crew:** 54
Draught: 4.2m (13ft 9in)	**Launch date:** 12 April 1929

ANGLER

SPECIFICATIONS

ANGLER

Displacement surfaced: **1854tnes (1825t)**	*Performance surfaced:* **20 knots**
Displacement submerged: **2448tnes (2410t)**	*Performance submerged:* **10 knots**
Machinery: **twin screws, diesels/electric motors; 5400/2740hp**	*Armament:* **10 533mm (21in) TT; one 76mm (3in) gun**
Length: **95m (311ft 9in)**	*Surface range:* **22,236km (12,000nm) at 10 knots**
Beam: **8.3m (27ft 3in)**	*Crew:* **80**
Draught: **4.6m (15ft 3in)**	*Launch date:* **4 July 1943**

The US submarine *Angler* was one of the massive Gato class of ocean-going submarines that played havoc with Japan's maritime commerce during the Pacific war, ending with the destruction of the merchant fleet. Under the command of Lt-Cdr Olsen, she opened her score in January 1944, when she sank a small freighter shortly after arriving in her operational area. Another freighter fell victim to *Angler*'s torpedoes in May, while the submarine was operating in the area of the Mandate Islands.

July 1944 found the boat operating off the Philippines and the Malay peninsula under a new skipper, Cdr Hess, who added another ship to the tally, followed by yet another in October.

After the war, together with many other Gato-class boats, *Angler* was rebuilt and given increased engine power and converted to the hunter-killer role. At the end of her operational life in 1963, her propellers were removed, her torpedo tubes welded shut, and she became an immobilized dockside training vessel (*AGSS*), employed to train Naval Reserve personnel. She was used in this role until the 1970s.

The Gato submarines, over 300 of which were built, represented the largest warship construction programme ever undertaken by the United States.

BARB

Another Gato class boat, the USS *Barb* (*SS20*) first operated in Atlantic waters, carrying out a reconnaissance of the Moroccan harbours of Rabat, Fedala, Casablanca, and Safi as well as Dakar in preparation for the Allied landings in North Africa, November 1942.

Transferred to the Pacific, with Lt-Cdr Waterman and Lt-Cdr Fluckey as successive captains, she enjoyed consistent success, and sank six ships in the waters between Formosa and Japan in March and May 1944. In September, *Barb*'s torpedoes claimed two ships totalling 15,906 tonnes (15,655 tons) as well as the 18,085-tonne (17,800-ton) Japanese escort carrier *Unyo*.

The submarine enjoyed further success in November 1944, sinking two ships of 15,505 tonnes (15,261 tons), and January 1945, when the skill of Lt-Cdr Fluckey and his crew sent another five ships to the bottom.

In July 1945, after sinking another enemy vessel with torpedoes, *Barb* made a rocket attack on Japanese positions on Kaihyo Island on the east coast of Karafuto in the Kuriles to the north of Japan; this was the first rocket operation by a submarine.

In 1955, as part of the NATO Mutual Aid Pact, *Barb* was assigned to the Italian Navy and renamed *Enrico Tazzoli*. She was discarded in 1973.

SPECIFICATIONS

BARB

Displacement surfaced: **1854tnes (1825t)**	*Performance surfaced:* **20 knots**
Displacement submerged: **2448tnes (2410t)**	*Performance submerged:* **10 knots**
Machinery: **twin screws, diesels/electric motors; 5400/2740hp**	*Armament:* **10 533mm (21in) TT; one 76mm (3in) gun**
Length: **95m (311ft 9in)**	*Surface range:* **22,236km (12,000nm) at 10 knots**
Beam: **8.3m (27ft 3in)**	*Crew:* **80**
Draught: **4.6m (15ft 3in)**	*Launch date:* **2 April 1942**

CUTLASS

SPECIFICATIONS

CUTLASS

Displacement surfaced: **1570tnes (1860t)**	*Performance surfaced:* **20 knots**
Displacement submerged: **2467tnes (2420t)**	*Performance submerged:* **10 knots**
Machinery: **twin screws, diesel/electric motors; 5400/2740hp**	*Armament:* **10 533mm (21in) torpedo tubes; two 150mm (5.9in) guns**
Length: **93.6m (307ft)**	*Surface range:* **22,518km (12,152nm) at 10 knots**
Beam: **8.3m (27ft 3in)**	*Crew:* **85**
Draught: **4.6m (15ft 3in)**	*Launch date:* **5 November 1944**

Commissioned in March 1945, the USS *Cutlass* belonged to the Tench class of some 50 boats, the last to be laid down in World War II in American yards. They incorporated many lessons learned from the operational use of the Gato-class boats, from which they were developed.

The Tench class were double-hulled ocean-going submarines, more strongly built than the Gatos and with an improved internal layout, which increased the displacement by some 40 tonnes (39 tons). About 20 of the boats were either cancelled or scrapped when partially completed at the point it was realized that Japan could no longer hope to win the war in the Pacific.

For the US Navy's submarine service, the war had begun in a rather downbeat fashion, with torpedoes that constantly failed to detonate and with a serious shortage of submarines, and had ended with the destruction of 1152 Japanese merchant ships of more than 508 tonnes (500 tons), amounting to nearly 5.08 million tonnes (five million tons).

The USS *Cutlass* remained on the US Navy's order of battle until 1973, when she was refurbished and transferred to Taiwan. Another boat, the *Diablo*, went to Pakistan and was sunk by surface forces in the 1971 Indo-Pakistan war.

DACE

One of the later Gato-class boats, USS *Dace* deployed to her operational area in the Pacific in June 1943, under Lt-Cdr McMahon. She sank a Japanese freighter on her first war patrol, but did not register another success until July 1944.

In October 1944, while deployed as part of a submarine group in support of the US landings at Leyte, she sank two ships totalling 13,149 tonnes (12,941 tons) and damaged a third.

A little later, her new commander (now Lt-Cdr Cleggett) brought his boat an even greater success when he attacked and sank the Japanese Takao class cruiser *Maya*.

Under a third skipper, Lt-Cdr Cole, she carried out minelaying operations in December, one enemy merchant ship being sunk as a result.

Dace finished her combat career by sinking a small freighter in Japanese waters in June 1945. After the end of the war she was completely refurbished and modernized, along with many other Gato boats, for delivery to NATO and other friendly navies.

Dace was assigned to the Italian Navy in December 1954 and named *Leonardo da Vinci*. She remained on the active list until well into the 1970s.

SPECIFICATIONS

DACE

Displacement surfaced: **1854tnes (1825t)**	*Performance surfaced:* **20 knots**
Displacement submerged: **2448tnes (2410t)**	*Performance submerged:* **10 knots**
Machinery: **twin screws, diesels/electric motors; 5400/2740hp**	*Armament:* **10 533mm (21in) TT; one 76mm (3in) gun**
Length: **95m (311ft 9in)**	*Surface range:* **22,236km (12,000nm) at 10 knots**
Beam: **8.3m (27ft 3in)**	*Crew:* **80**
Draught: **4.6m (15ft 3in)**	*Launch date:* **25 April 1943**

DRUM

SPECIFICATIONS

DRUM

Displacement surfaced: **1854tnes (1825t)**	*Performance surfaced:* **20 knots**
Displacement submerged: **2448tnes (2410t)**	*Performance submerged:* **10 knots**
Machinery: **twin screws, diesels/electric motors; 5400/2740hp**	*Armament:* **10 533mm (21in) TT; one 76mm (3in) gun**
Length: **95m (311ft 9in)**	*Surface range:* **22,236km (12,000nm) at 10 knots**
Beam: **8.3m (27ft 3in)**	*Crew:* **80**
Draught: **4.6m (15ft 3in)**	*Launch date:* **15 May 1941**

The USS *Drum* was without doubt one of the most successful American submarines of the Pacific War. On her first deployment, in April 1942, she sank two freighters and the Japanese seaplane carrier *Mizuho* off Japan, and in the following weeks she operated in support of the American defence of Midway Island.

August 1942 found her in the waters off Truk, covering the US landings on Guadalcanal, and between September and October she sank three ships totalling 13,420 tonnes (13,208 tons). In December, her first captain (Lt-Cdr Rice) having handed over to Lt-Cdr McMahon, she torpedoed and damaged the Japanese light carrier *Ryuho*.

After an overhaul, she returned to operational duty in the summer of 1943, sinking another ship in September and one in November. Her torpedoes claimed three more enemy vessels, with another damaged, in October 1944.

During this time there were no fewer than 54 American submarines operating in Japanese waters; by way of contrast, the Japanese could only deploy one boat, the *I-21*, to distant waters, operating between Hawaii and the US west coast.

Drum served until 1962, when she became a reserve training vessel and eventually a museum exhibit.

GATO

Among the first of her class assigned to the US Pacific Fleet, *Gato* departed New London 16 February 1942 for Pearl Harbor via the Panama Canal and San Francisco. On her first war patrol from Pearl Harbor (20 April–10 June 1942), she unsuccessfully attacked a converted aircraft carrier before being driven away by fierce depth-charging off the Marshalls. *Gato*'s first major operational mission was to form part of a submarine screen to the northwest of Midway Island, guarding against a possible Japanese landing. It was to be more than six months before she got her first taste of offensive action, but in January 1943, under Lt-Cdr Foley, she sank four ships totalling 13,205 tonnes (12,997 tons) and damaged four more. She claimed her next victim in November 1943, followed by another in December.

In February 1944, during large-scale offensive air and sea operations around the Caroline Islands, *Gato* sank three more freighters and three small craft while covering the exit channels from the island of Truk. There were further successes in February 1945, when *Gato* (now under Lt-Cdr Farrell) sank a freighter and a corvette.

Gato, along with all the early boats of her class, was laid up at the end of the Pacific war to await disposal in various ways. *Gato*, which was built by the Electric Boat Company, was discarded in 1960.

SPECIFICATIONS

GATO

Displacement surfaced: **1854tnes (1825t)**	*Performance surfaced:* **20 knots**
Displacement submerged: **2448tnes (2410t)**	*Performance submerged:* **10 knots**
Machinery: **twin screws, diesels/electric motors; 5400/2740hp**	*Armament:* **10 533mm (21in) TT; one 76mm (3in) gun**
Length: **95m (311ft 9in)**	*Surface range:* **22,236km (12,000nm) at 10 knots**
Beam: **8.3m (27ft 3in)**	*Crew:* **80**
Draught: **4.6m (15ft 3in)**	*Launch date:* **21 August 1941**

LIZARDFISH

SPECIFICATIONS

LIZARDFISH

Displacement surfaced: **1854tnes (1825t)**	Performance surfaced: **20 knots**
Displacement submerged: **2448tnes (2410t)**	Performance submerged: **10 knots**
Machinery: **twin screws, diesels/electric motors; 5400/2740hp**	Armament: **10 533mm (21in) TT; one 76mm (3in) gun**
Length: **95m (311ft 9in)**	Surface range: **22,236km (12,000nm) at 10 knots**
Beam: **8.3m (27ft 3in)**	Crew: **80**
Draught: **4.6m (15ft 3in)**	Launch date: **16 July 1944**

The USS *Lizardfish* (*SS373*) was one of the last of the Gato-class boats to be built by the Manitowoc shipyard. In July 1945 she deployed to the Southeast Asia theatre, where she and other American submarines operated alongside British boats in mopping up the last Japanese vessels in the area. In the course of these operations, under Cdr Butler, she sank a Japanese submarine chaser. It was during these operations that *Lizardfish*'s sister boat, *Bluefish* (Lt-Cdr Forbes), sank the Japanese seaplane support submarine *I-351*, the only one of her type to be completed.

Late construction boats such as *Lizardfish* were completed with alternative gun mountings fore and aft of the tower, and some were fitted with rocket launchers for shore bombardment (as submarines could approach targets submerged and therefore unseen).

Fully refurbished and improved after World War II, *Lizardfish* remained on the US Navy's active list until January 1962, when she was transferred to the Italian Navy as the *Evangelista Torricelli*.

She was no longer operational by 1970, but was still being used for training and experimental tasks. She was discarded in 1976.

During the 1960s the Italian Navy used nine ex-American ocean-going submarines.

MARLIN

The *Marlin* (*SS205*) and her sister submarine, *Mackerel* (*SS204*) were small, experimental coastal craft built at the request of the US Navy's leading submarine expert, Admiral T.C. Hart, who was conscious of the urgent need to find an effective replacement for the ageing S-type boats and who held the opinion that the ocean-going fleet boats were becoming too large (as in other navies).

Hart's notion that smaller vessels – optimized for the defence of strategic naval bases such as Pearl Harbor and key points like the Panama Canal – should be the subject of a priority building programme, was strongly opposed by other senior US Navy personnel, especially submariners, who knew the importance of deploying large, well-armed, long-range underwater craft that were capable of paralyzing Japan's maritime commerce in distant waters.

Despite the objections, the two boats were built to an Electric Boat Company design; but although they performed well they never saw operational service and were ultimately scrapped. However, six modified boats, fitted with updated equipment, were built for Peru after World War II had ended.

Marlin and *Mackerel* were broken up in 1946 and 1947, respectively.

SPECIFICATIONS

MARLIN

Displacement surfaced: **955tnes (940t)**	*Performance surfaced:* **16.5 knots**
Displacement submerged: **1158tnes (1140t)`**	*Performance submerged:* **8 knots**
Machinery: **two screws, diesel engines; 1680hp**	*Armament:* **six 533mm (21in) TT; one 76mm (3in) gun**
Length: **72.82m (238ft 11in)**	*Surface range:* **4632km (2500nm)**
Beam: **6.60m (21ft 8in)**	*Crew:* **80**
Draught: **3.96m (13ft)**	*Launch date:* **29 January 1941**

NAUTILUS

SPECIFICATIONS

NAUTILUS

Displacement surfaced: **2773tnes (2730t)**	Performance surfaced: **17 knots**
Displacement submerged: **3962tnes (3900t)**	Performance submerged: **8 knots**
Machinery: **twin screws, diesel/electric motors; 5450/2540hp**	Armament: **six 533mm (21in) torpedo tubes, two 152mm (6in) guns**
Length: **113m (370ft)**	Surface range: **18,350km (10,000nm)**
Beam: **10m (33ft 3in)**	Crew: **90**
Draught: **4.8m (15ft 9in)**	Launch date: **15 March 1930**

Formerly designated *V-6*, the USS *Nautilus* and her sister boat, *Narwhal*, were designed as long-range ocean-going cruiser submarines and were virtually identical to the US Navy's sole minelaying submarine, *Argonaut*, except that stern torpedo tubes replaced her minelaying tubes.

In 1940 she was re-fitted as a tanker submarine, the idea being that she would make an ocean or island rendezvous with long-range reconnaissance aircraft (an idea subsequently adopted by the Japanese).

In 1941 both *Nautilus* and *Narwhal* received new engines, and although *Nautilus* was deployed for offensive operations from time to time, her main function throughout the war, mainly because of her long range, was special operations.

In August 1942, for example, both *Nautilus* and *Argonaut* landed a raiding force on Makin, in the Gilbert Islands. In October 1942 she sank two merchant ships in Japanese waters, and in May the following year she and *Narwhal* acted as marker submarines for US marine forces moving in to recapture Attu, in the Aleutian Islands. In March 1944 *Nautilus* sank another large merchant ship off the Mandate Islands. Both *Nautilus* and *Narwhal* were scrapped in 1945.

TANG

One of the few Gato-class boats built by the Mare Island Naval Dockyard, the USS *Tang* had the dubious distinction of going down in history as the submarine that sank herself.

Commanded by Lt-Cdr O'Kane, she began her operational life in February 1944 during Operation Hailstone, the offensive air/sea strikes in the area of the Caroline Islands, when she sank one freighter. During April 1944, operating in support of US carrier forces attacking Japanese-held islands, she rescued 22 shot-down American pilots, sometimes penetrating into the Truk Lagoon to do so under extremely hazardous conditions, a feat that brought Lt-Cdr O'Kane a deserved Medal of Honor.

In June 1944, while operating off Japan, Formosa and the Kuriles, she sank 10 ships totalling 39,787 tonnes (39,159 tons), an impressive result by any standard. She claimed three more Japanese merchant ships in August. In October, operating in the Formosa Strait – an area rich in enemy merchant traffic – she sank another six ships totalling 19,559 tonnes (19,250 tons) in attacks on convoys, as well as torpedoing and damaging two more.

Tang was sunk by one of her own torpedoes, which went out of control and circled her before impacting.

SPECIFICATIONS

TANG

Displacement surfaced: **1854tnes (1825t)**	Performance surfaced: **20 knots**
Displacement submerged: **2448tnes (2410t)**	Performance submerged: **10 knots**
Machinery: **twin screws, diesel/electric motors; 5400/2740hp**	Armament: **10 533mm (21in) TT; one 76mm (3in) gun**
Length: **95m (311ft 9in)**	Surface range: **22,236km (12,000nm) at 10 knots**
Beam: **8.3m (27ft 3in)**	Crew: **80**
Draught: **4.6m (15ft 3in)**	Launch date: **17 August 1943**

TAUTOG

Built by the Electric Boat Company, the Tambor-class submarine USS *Tautog* sank 26 ships during World War II, the biggest toll exacted by any enemy submarine. She was at Pearl Harbor at the time of the Japanese attack on 7 December 1941, but escaped undamaged.

Under Lt-Cdr Willingham, she opened her score in April 1942, sinking two ships in Japanese waters and the submarine *I-28* off Truk, the latter as she was recovering midget submarines.

October 1942, after further successes, found her laying mines off the coast of Indo-China and in the Gulf of Siam, and she opened the new year of 1943 with two more sinkings, her skipper now being Lt-Cdr Sieglaff. In April, she sank another merchantman and the Japanese destroyer *Isonami*.

In January 1944 she repeated her exploit of the previous new year by sinking two more ships, and in March she claimed four more victims, all off Japan. In May 1944, with Lt-Cdr Baskett in command, she sank four more ships, followed by another three in July. Following her new year precedent, she closed her scoreboard by sinking three more transports in January 1945.

Tautog was scrapped in 1960, an ignominious end for a gallant submarine.

TENCH

Although the USS *Tench* had a brief operational career, it was a spectacular one. In May 1945, under the command of Lt-Cdr Baskett – formerly of the USS *Tautog* – she sank six Japanese ships in Japanese waters.

The Tench class boats were improved Gatos, although the external differences were so minor that sometimes no distinction is made between the two. By the time *Tench* became operational in 1945, the Imperial Japanese Navy suffered an almost complete lack of dedicated anti-submarine warfare escort vessels, their destroyers having been expended in fruitless and costly air and surface actions, or torpedoed by submarines.

As a consequence, US submarines were able to run riot in the closing months of the Pacific war, roving at will in Japanese waters. Towards the end of the war, major Japanese surface units were forced to remain penned up in their harbours, where they were subjected to constant air attack.

The majority of the Tench class submarines were cancelled or scrapped incomplete as the war approached its end. At the end of her active life, *Tench* was transferred to the Peruvian Navy in 1976, to be used for spare parts.

SPECIFICATIONS

TENCH

Displacement surfaced: **1570tnes (1860t)**	*Performance surfaced:* **20 knots**
Displacement submerged: **2467tnes (2420t)**	*Performance submerged:* **10 knots**
Machinery: **twin screws, diesel/electric motors; 5400/2740hp**	*Armament:* **10 533mm (21in) torpedo tubes; two 150mm (5.9in) guns**
Length: **93.6m (307ft)**	*Surface range:* **22,518km (12,152nm) at 10 knots**
Beam: **8.3m (27ft 3in)**	*Crew:* **85**
Draught: **4.6m (15ft 3in)**	*Launch date:* **7 July 1944**

D3

SPECIFICATIONS

D3

Displacement surfaced: **948tnes (933t)**	*Performance surfaced:* **14 knots**
Displacement submerged: **1376tnes (1354t)**	*Performance submerged:* **9 knots**
Machinery: **twin screws, diesel/electric motors; 2600/1600hp**	*Armament:* **eight 533mm (21in) TT; one 100mm (3.9in) gun**
Length: **76m (249ft 4in)**	*Surface range:* **13,897km (7500nm) at 12 knots**
Beam: **6.5m (21ft 4in)**	*Crew:* **80**
Draught: **3.8m (12ft 6in)**	*Launch date:* **12 July 1929**

The Russian submarine *D3*, a Series I boat, was serving with the Northern Fleet at the time of Germany's attack on the Soviet Union in June 1941, and deployed to her war station of Norway's North Cape.

On 27 September, commanded by Lt-Cdr F.V. Konstantinov (and with the commander of the 2nd Submarine Division, Capt 2nd Class I.A. Kolyshkin on board) she began a series of attacks on German convoys off the Norwegian coast. All her torpedoes missed their targets. The same thing happened in December, by which time Konstantinov had been replaced Lt-Cdr N.A. Bibeyev.

Bibeyev's aim against the German minelayer *Brummer*, which *D3* attacked on 14 March 1942, was equally as poor, and attacks on German convoys in June 1942 also met with no success. The boat failed to return from a mission in July 1942, presumably sunk by a mine barrage.

The Series I submarines were good seaboats, but their construction was of poor quality and they had a number of design faults. Their diving time, originally, was three minutes, and much work had to be done on the ballast tanks before this was reduced to 30 seconds. Of the six boats in the class, four became war casualties.

D4

Three of Russia's D-class submarines, one of them *D4*, served in the Black Sea during World War II. From May to July 1942, she and all the other submarines assigned to the Black Sea Fleet carried out 77 supply missions to the besieged fortress of Sevastopol, under heavy attack by the Germans. *D4* herself carried out five.

In the summer of 1943, under Lt-Cdr Gremyako, *D4* was assigned to patrol the supply route between Sevastopol, now in German hands, and Constanza in Romania. On 11 August, *D4* sank the 6796-tonne (6689-ton) steamer *Boj Feddersen*, and on 20 August the steamer *Varna*.

Italian midget submarines were active at this time in the hunter-killer role, and on 28 August one of them sank the *Shch 207*. *D4* was sunk on 4 December 1943 by the German sub-chasers *UJ103* and *UJ102* with a barrage of depth-charges.

Of the other two D-class boats deployed in the Black Sea, *D6* was damaged by air attack 96km (60 miles) west of Sevastopol on 18 August 1941; she was subsequently totally destroyed by aerial attack and fire damage while in dry dock at Sevastopol on 12 November 1941.

The third boat, *D5*, performed excellent service and survived the war, being discarded in the 1950s.

SPECIFICATIONS

D4

Displacement surfaced: **948tnes (933t)**	*Performance surfaced:* **14 knots**
Displacement submerged: **1376tnes (1354t)**	*Performance submerged:* **9 knots**
Machinery: **twin screws, diesel/electric motors; 2600/1600hp**	*Armament:* **eight 533mm (21in) TT; one 100mm (3.9in) gun**
Length: **76m (249ft 4in)**	*Surface range:* **13,897km (7500nm) at 12 knots**
Beam: **6.5m (21ft 4in)**	*Crew:* **80**
Draught: **3.8m (12ft 6in)**	*Launch date:* **1929**

K3

SPECIFICATIONS

K3

Displacement surfaced:
 1514tnes (1490t)

Displacement submerged:
 2138tnes (2104t)

Machinery:
 twin screws,
 diesel/electric motors;
 8400/2400hp

Length:
 97.65m (320ft 4in)

Beam:
 7.4m (24ft 3in)

Draught:
 4.51m (14ft 10in)

Performance surfaced:
 21 knots

Performance submerged:
 10 knots

Armament:
 10 533mm (21in) TT;
 two 100mm (3.9in)
 guns; 20 mines

Surface range:
 22,236km (12,000nm)
 at 9 knots

Crew:
 60

Launch date:
 1938

The Series XIV submarine *K3* was one of 12 K-class ocean-going submarines that were developed from several previous proposed designs. The boats were heavily armed, and were intended to carry a small dismantled reconnaissance floatplane known as SPL (*Samolet dlya Podvodnoi Lodki* – aircraft for submarines) which was actually built and test flown, but never entered service.

K3 was in the Baltic at the time of the German invasion, and in August 1941 was transferred to the Northern Fleet via the Stalin (White Sea) Canal, reaching Molotovsk on 25 September. In November, she laid mine barrages off the Norwegian coast, after which she made a number of abortive attacks on German convoys. During one of these, on 26 November, she was attacked by German sub-chasers and depth-charged, being forced to surface. She beat off the German craft in a gun duel, sinking one of them (*UJ1708*). In February 1943, *K3* sank another sub-chaser, together with a large transport.

On 21 March 1943, after making two abortive attacks on enemy convoys, *K3* was attacked by a group of three sub-chasers and sunk. Her commander throughout most of her operational career was Capt 3rd Class Malofeyev.

K21

Like her sister vessel *K3*, *K21* was transferred from the Baltic to the Northern Fleet via Lake Ladoga and the White Sea Canal in August 1941, arriving in September. Her first operational sorties involved laying mine barrages.

In June 1942, operating as part of a force attempting to cover Russian convoys QP.13 and the ill-fated PQ.17, her commander (Captain 2nd Class Lunin) made an unsuccessful attack on the German battleship *Tirpitz*, and in August she attacked a force of German minelayers, again without result.

On 18 February 1943, still under Lunin, she laid a mine barrage off Norway, disembarked some agents and fired six torpedoes into Bogen Bay, where enemy vessels were concentrated, but failed to hit anything. In December of that year, she was deployed against the battlecruiser *Scharnhorst*, which was sunk by the Royal Navy in the Battle of North Cape.

K21 survived the war and remained in service until 1959, when she was decommissioned for use as a permanent training unit at the Polyarnoye naval base. Although the K class boats were among the best available to the Soviet Navy in World War II, they were seldom handled properly and failed to produce the results of which they were capable.

SPECIFICATIONS

K21

Displacement surfaced: 1514tnes (1490t)	**Performance surfaced:** 21 knots
Displacement submerged: 2138tnes (2104t)	**Performance submerged:** 10 knots
Machinery: twin screws, diesel/electric motors; 8400/2400hp	**Armament:** 10 533mm (21in) TT; two 100mm (3.9in) guns; 20 mines
Length: 97.65m (320ft 4in)	**Surface range:** 22,236km (12,000nm) at 9 knots
Beam: 7.4m (24ft 3in)	**Crew:** 60
Draught: 4.51m (14ft 10in)	**Launch date:** 1938

L3

SPECIFICATIONS

L3

Displacement surfaced: **1219tnes (1200t)**	*Performance surfaced:* **15 knots**
Displacement submerged: **1574tnes (1550t)**	*Performance submerged:* **9 knots**
Powerplant: **twin screws, diesel/electric motors; 2200/1050hp**	*Armament:* **six 533mm (21in) TT; one 100mm (3.9in) gun**
Length: **81m (265ft 9in)**	*Surface range:* **9265km (5000nm)**
Beam: **7.5m (24ft 7in)**	*Crew:* **54**
Draught: **7.8m (15ft 9in)**	*Launch date:* **July 1931**

The *L3* was one of six Series II L-class submarines. The boats were modelled on the British submarine *L55*, which had been sunk by Russian destroyers off Kronstadt in June 1919 and later raised.

L3 was in the Baltic at the start of the Russian campaign, and one of her first tasks was minelaying. In August 1942 she was part of a wave of Soviet submarines that broke through the mine barrages laid by German and Finnish naval forces in the Gulf of Finland; these boats began a series of heavy attacks on German supply vessels, *L3* sinking a steamer and probably sinking another. During this period *L3* was commanded by Capt 2nd Class Grischenko.

The onset of winter brought a halt to operations, and when *L3* returned to action minelaying was her main activity. By late 1944 she was once again preying on German transport vessels which, when 1945 began, were mostly involved in evacuating German troops and civilians from East Prussia.

On the night of 16/17 April 1945, *L3* attacked the German steamship *Goya*, which was crowded with refugees. More than 6000 people lost their lives.

L3 survived the war; she was renumbered *B3* in 1945, and was decommissioned and scrapped at Kronstadt between 1959 and 1960.

M172

O riginally numbered *M88*, *M172* was a Series XII boat, part of the third batch of M-class small coastal submarines designed to be easily transported by rail in a fully assembled condition.

M172's war operations began with patrols off the Norwegian Polar Coast in July 1941, under the command of Lt-Cdr I.I. Fisanovich, and she opened her score on 12 September 1941 by sinking a small coaster. In May 1942 she came close to being destroyed when she was subjected to an eight-hour depth-charge attack by German submarine chasers, the latter vessels only breaking off when they came under heavy fire from Soviet coastal batteries.

Early in February 1943 *M172* sank a German patrol boat, and during the first months of the year she was involved in a succession of abortive attacks on German convoys along the Polar Coast. Further attacks in September and October 1943 were also conspicuous by their failure, and *M172* failed to return from one such war patrol, possibly lost on one of the flanking mine barrages laid out by the Germans during the summer months. A sister boat, *M174*, was also lost at the same time and in similar circumstances.

Some M-class boats were shipped to the Black Sea in 1944 to harass the German withdrawal.

SPECIFICATIONS

M172

Displacement surfaced: **209tnes (206t)**	*Performance surfaced:* **14 knots**
Displacement submerged: **221tnes (218t)**	*Performance submerged:* **8 knots**
Machinery: **single screw, diesel/electric motors; 800/400hp**	*Armament:* **two 533mm (21in) TT; one 45mm gun**
Length: **44.5m (146ft)**	*Surface range:* **3484km (1880nm) at 8 knots**
Beam: **3.3m (10ft 10in)**	*Crew:* **20**
Draught: **3m (9ft 10in)**	*Launch date:* **1936**

M201

SPECIFICATIONS

M201

Displacement surfaced: **285tnes (281t)**	Performance surfaced: **15.7 knots**
Displacement submerged: **357tnes (351t)**	Performance submerged: **8 knots**
Machinery: **twin screws, diesel/electric motors; 1600/875hp**	Armament: **one 533mm (21in) TT; one 45mm gun**
Length: **49.5m (162ft 5in)**	Surface range: **3484km (1880nm) at 8 knots**
Beam: **4.4m (14ft 5in)**	Crew: **24**
Draught: **2.75m (9ft)**	Launch date: **1940**

The *M201*, a Series XV boat of new design, was under construction at Leningrad when the city came under threat from the advancing Germans in July 1941. The *M201* was evacuated incomplete via Russia's mighty inland waterways to Astrakhan, on the Caspian Sea, for completion.

In April 1943 she set out on the same route, but in reverse, and joined the Northern Fleet in June, beginning patrols off Varangerfjord before the end of the year. Her captain at this time was Lt-Cdr Balin. The latter had bad luck, missing contact with German convoys on two occasions in February 1944 and another one in May.

In June, *M201* joined *S14*, *S104* and *M200* in a combined operation against German convoy traffic off northern Norway. On the 20th, Balin had just got into a good position to attack a convoy when he was sighted by a Heinkel 115 floatplane and forced to dive, being heavily attacked by four German submarine chasers, but she got away. Balin's chance finally came in August 1944, when *M201* closed in and sank the German escort vessel *V6112* off Persfjord, in the light of the midnight sun.

M201 survived the war and was transferred to the Baltic via the White Sea Canal in 1948.

S7

For the crew of the Series IXbis submarine *S7*, operations began on 22 June 1941 with a reconnaissance mission off Gotland. On 26 September, under Capt 3rd Class L.P. Lisin, *S7* sank a small steamer off the Swedish coast. In November, she was involved in special operations, disembarking agents in Narva Bay, Estonia, and on convoy protection duty.

Her first real success on offensive operations came in June and July 1942, when she sank four ships totalling 9311 tonnes (9164 tons); three of these were Swedish, which the Russians regarded as fair game as they were transporting raw materials to Germany.

In September 1942, having broken through enemy mine barrages with a number of other submarines, *S7* was operating in the Aaland Sea, between the Baltic and the Gulf of Bothnia. On 21 October 1942, she was sunk by the Finnish submarine *Vesihiisi* (Lt-Cdr Aittola). Four Russians survived, including Capt Lisin, and were taken prisoner.

The S-class boats to which *S7* belonged were medium-sized submarines designed for open sea warfare, and were built in three progressively improved types. In general appearance, the third series, the Type XVI, resembled the German Type VIIC U-boat.

SPECIFICATIONS

S7

Displacement surfaced: **870tnes (856t)**	*Performance surfaced:* **18.75 knots**
Displacement submerged: **1107tnes (1090t)**	*Performance submerged:* **8.8 knots**
Machinery: **twin screws, diesel/electric motors; 4000/1100hp**	*Armament:* **six 533mm (21in) TT; one 100mm (3.9in) gun**
Length: **77.5m (255ft 1in)**	*Surface range:* **16,677km (9000nm) at 10.5 knots**
Beam: **6.4m (21ft)**	*Crew:* **46**
Draught: **4.06m (13ft 4in)**	*Launch date:* **1937**

S13

SPECIFICATIONS

S13

Displacement surfaced: **870tnes (856t)**	*Performance surfaced:* **18.75 knots**
Displacement submerged: **1107tnes (1090t)**	*Performance submerged:* **8.8 knots**
Machinery: **two screws, diesel/electric motors; 4000/1100hp**	*Armament:* **six 533mm (21in) TT; one 100mm (3.9in) gun**
Length: **77.5m (255ft 1in)**	*Surface range:* **16,677km (9000nm) at 10.5 knots**
Beam: **6.4m (21ft)**	*Crew:* **46**
Draught: **4.06m (13ft 4in)**	*Launch date:* **1941**

The Type IXbis submarine *S13*'s war began in August 1942 when, commanded by Lt-Cdr Malanchenko, she sank two freighters totalling 3767 tonnes (3704 tons) in the Baltic. On 15 October, operating in Finnish waters, she survived a depth-charge attack by submarine-chasers, but sustained damage that put her out of action for some time.

Her period of real success began in September 1944, when – now under the command of Capt 3rd Class Marinesko – she began offensive operations against German supply and evacuation traffic. On 30 January 1945, when on station 52km (28nm) NNE of Leba, East Prussia, she attacked the 25,893-tonne (25,484-ton) passenger liner *Wilhelm Gustloff*, which was sailing without an escort. The submarine fired a salvo of four torpedoes, three of which found their mark. The liner sank with the loss of some 5200 lives, mostly civilian refugees. Then, on 10 February, still cruising in the same area, *S13* sighted the 14,895-tonne (14,660-ton) passenger ship *General Steuben* and sank her with one hit. Because of the freezing temperature of the water, escort vessels were only able to rescue about 300 of the 3000 persons who had been on board.

S13, the most successful of all Soviet submarines, was decommissioned and scrapped between 1958 and 1959.

S56

The Soviet submarine *S56* had to travel a long way to reach her war station in the Arctic. In October 1942, along with other boats that had been assigned to the Pacific Fleet, she sailed from Petropavlovsk, Kamchatka via Dutch Harbour, San Francisco and the Panama Canal to Halifax, Nova Scotia. From there, *S56*, *S55* and *S54* sailed to Rosyth, Scotland, and then on to the Kola Inlet, which they reached in March 1943.

Her war operations began with patrols off the Norwegian coast in April, and on 17 May, commanded by Capt 3rd Class Shchedrin, she sank the tanker *Eurostadt* and torpedoed a large freighter, but the missile failed to explode.

In July, *S56* sank the minesweeper *M346* and a patrol boat, and in January 1944 she sank the 5080-tonne (5000-ton) freighter *Henrietta Schulte*. In further operations the Soviet boat was not so successful, and on 26 September 1944, while attempting to attack German minesweepers, she was damaged in a depth-charge attack, effectively bringing her wartime career to an end, though not her sailing life.

S56 returned to the Pacific via the Northern Route in the summer of 1950. She was decommissioned in 1959, and became a stationary submarine training unit at the naval base at Vladivostok.

SPECIFICATIONS

S56

Displacement surfaced: **870tnes (856t)**	*Performance surfaced:* **18.75 knots**
Displacement submerged: **1107tnes (1090t)**	*Performance submerged:* **8.8 knots**
Machinery: **twin screws, diesel/electric motors; 4000/1100hp**	*Armament:* **six 533mm (21in) TT; one 100mm (3.9in) gun**
Length: **77.5m (255ft 1in)**	*Surface range:* **16,677km (9000nm) at 10.5 knots**
Beam: **6.4m (21ft)**	*Crew:* **46**
Draught: **4.06m (13ft 4in)**	*Launch date:* **December 1939**

SHCH 307

SPECIFICATIONS

SHCH 307

Displacement surfaced: **595tnes (586t)**	Performance surfaced: **14 knots**
Displacement submerged: **713tnes (702t)**	Performance submerged: **8 knots**
Machinery: **two screws; diesel/electric motors; 1600/800hp**	Armament: **six 533mm (21in) TT; two 45mm (1.7in) guns**
Length: **58.5m (191ft 11in)**	Surface range: **1667km (900nm) at 8.5 knots**
Beam: **6.2m (20ft 4in)**	Crew: **40**
Draught: **4.3m (14ft 1in)**	Launch date: **1 August 1934**

The Shch series of submarines (Shch is an abbreviation of *Shchuka* or Pike) were developed from a 1920s design and were constructed from 1933 until after World War II.

On 28 July 1941, with Lt-Cdr Petrov in charge, *Shch 307* enjoyed an early success when she sank the German submarine *U-144* in the Gulf of Finland. In August, along with other Russian naval units, she was forced to withdraw from Tallin (Estonia) to the main Soviet naval base of Kronstadt as the German armies pushed east, where she remained penned up until September 1942, when she joined the mass breakout into the Baltic through the enemy mine barrages.

In the following weeks, now with Capt 3rd Class Momot in command, *Shch 307* sank one ship and missed three others, and had no further success before she was forced to return to Kronstadt because of ice in November. She fared no better under a new skipper Lt-Cdr Kalinin, when she again broke out in the summer of 1944, missing six targets in rapid succession. Two more misses, in January 1945, brought a less than successful war career to a close.

Shch 307 was scrapped between 1958 and 1959, but her conning tower was preserved at the submarine training school.

SHCH 317

The combat debut of the *Shch 317* occurred in December 1939, during the 'Winter War' with Finland. On 7 December, the Soviet Union declared the Finnish coast from Tornio to Helsinki a blockade zone, later including the Aaland Islands between the Baltic and the Gulf of Bothnia. Five submarines were deployed, including *Shch 317*. One of them (*S1*) sank the German steamer *Bolheim*, and another (*Shch 323*) the Estonian steamer *Kassari*.

In October 1941, *Shch 317* attacked the German light cruiser *Leipzig* in the Baltic, but failed to hit her. However in June 1942, under the command of Lt-Cdr Mokhov, she sank four ships totalling 8416 tonnes (8283 tons) and narrowly missed another.

There was to be no chance of repeating this success. On 12 July 1942, while returning from a war patrol with the Divisional Commander (Capt 3rd Class Egorov) on board, she was attacked repeatedly over a three-day period by German and Finnish submarine-chasers as she passed between two mine barrages. It is not known whether she succumbed to their depth-charges or to the minefields, but she never reached her base. By the beginning of 1943, extensive minefields were making it extremely hazardous for Russian submarines, especially in coastal waters.

SPECIFICATIONS

SHCH 317

Displacement surfaced: **595tnes (586t)**	*Performance surfaced:* **14 knots**
Displacement submerged: **713tnes (702t)**	*Performance submerged:* **8 knots**
Machinery: **twin screws; diesel/electric motors; 1600/800hp**	*Armament:* **six 533mm (21in) TT; two 45mm (1.7in) guns**
Length: **58.5m (191ft 11in)**	*Surface range:* **1667km (900nm) at 8.5 knots**
Beam: **6.2m (20ft 4in)**	*Crew:* **40**
Draught: **4.3m (14ft 1in)**	*Launch date:* **25 September 1935**

INDEX

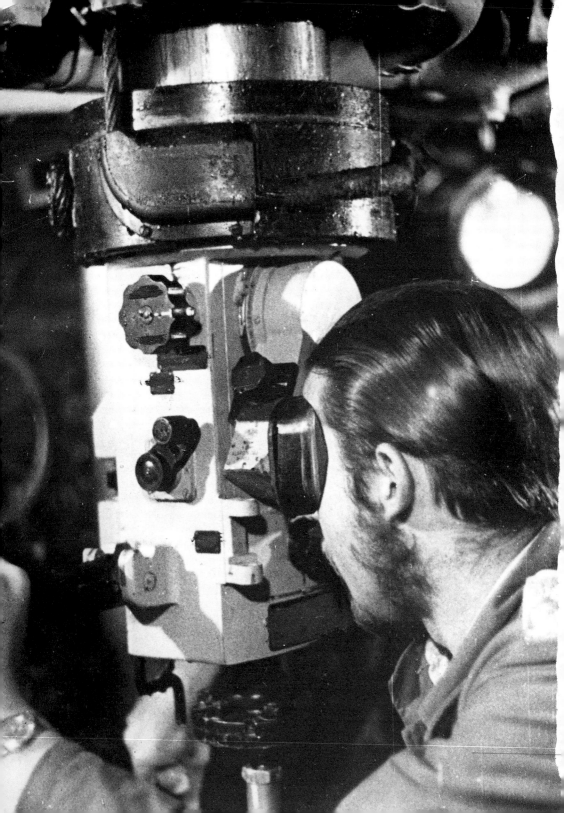